Private History
in Public

ABOUT THE SERIES
The American Association for State and Local History Book Series publishes technical and professional information for those who practice and support history, and addresses issues critical to the field of state and local history. To submit a proposal or manuscript to the series, please request proposal guidelines from AASLH headquarters: AASLH Book Series, 1717 Church St., Nashville, Tennessee 37203. Telephone: (615) 320-3203. Fax: (615) 327-9013. Web site: www.aaslh.org.

ABOUT THE ORGANIZATION
The American Association for State and Local History (AASLH) is a non-profit educational organization dedicated to advancing knowledge, understanding, and appreciation of local history in the United States and Canada. In addition to sponsorship of this book series, the Association publishes the periodical *History News*, a newsletter, technical leaflets and reports, and other materials; confers prizes and awards in recognition of outstanding achievement in the field; and supports a broad education program and other activities designed to help members work more effectively. To join the organization, contact: Membership Director, AASLH, 1717 Church St., Nashville, Tennessee 37203.

Private History in Public

Exhibition and the Settings of Everyday Life

Tammy S. Gordon

A Division of
ROWMAN & LITTLEFIELD PUBLISHERS, INC.
Lanham • New York • Toronto • Plymouth, UK

Published by AltaMira Press
A division of Rowman & Littlefield Publishers, Inc.
A wholly owned subsidiary of The Rowman & Littlefield Publishing Group, Inc.
4501 Forbes Boulevard, Suite 200, Lanham, Maryland 20706
http://www.altamirapress.com

Estover Road, Plymouth PL6 7PY, United Kingdom

British Library Cataloguing in Publication Information Available

Library of Congress Cataloging-in-Publication Data
Stone-Gordon, Tammy.
  Private history in public : exhibition and the settings of everyday life / Tammy S.
Gordon.
     p. cm.
  Includes bibliographical references and index.
  ISBN 978-0-7591-1934-5 (cloth : alk. paper) — ISBN 978-0-7591-1935-2 (pbk. :
alk. paper) — ISBN 978-0-7591-1936-9 (electronic)
  1. Historical museums—Exhibitions. 2. Public history—United States. 3. Public
history—Canada. 4. Historical museums—Social aspects—United States. 5.
Historical museums—Social aspects—Canada. 6. United States—History, Local—
Philosophy. 7. Canada—History, Local—Philosophy. I. Title.
  D2.5.S76 2010
  973.075—dc22   2009031150

Printed in the United States of America

To Chris, Josefina, Max, and my mentor, Juan.

Contents

Foreword   ix

Acknowledgments   xiii

1   Historical Display, Commerce, and Community   1

2   Toward a New Typology of Historical Exhibition in the
United States   15

3   Community Exhibition: History, Identity, and Dialogue   33

4   Entrepreneurial Exhibition: Historical Display and the
Small Business Tradition   59

5   Vernacular Exhibition and the Business of History   75

6   Local History, Global Economy: The Functions of History
Exhibits in the Settings of Everyday Life   97

Notes   117

Bibliography   137

Index   149

About the Author   153

Foreword

Interest in the past is booming. The History Channel remains one of the most successful cable channels. Historians such as David McCullough, Stephen Ambrose, and Doris Kearns Goodwin, along with historical documentarian Ken Burns, have become celebrities and their books and films enjoy a wide following.

An even more vivid reminder of our continuing interest in the past is the advent of scrapbooking as a hobby. Ten years ago scrapbooking hardly registered as an activity; today a Google search comes up with almost 20,000,000 mentions. Scrapbooking should be of great interest to those of us in the history museum field. It is, in fact, a synonym for the creation of a personal or family history museum, an intimate record of important stories, personalities, experiences, and artifacts to be preserved and interpreted by both its creators and successive generations. It is private history for private use, but in the future it may be a valuable source of public history.

And at the same time, history museums, historic sites, and historic houses--the official collectors, preservers, and interpreters of our past--are in decline. A reasonable question to ask is, Why? Part of the answer can be found in the pages of this book.

One of the great success stories of the American museum movement has been the professionalization of museum work and especially the professionalization of the exhibit-making process, still the primary point of engagement between museum creator and museum user. The model of antiquarian displays of venerated artifacts with personalized and idiosyncratic labels has been replaced by a model of thematic exhibitions with a gloss of clean and well-laid-out casework and labels designed with specific educational outcomes for carefully targeted audiences whose interests have been plotted through rigorous audience research. The result of all this has been exhibitions that have a high level of intellectual rigor, a look and feel that exudes professionalism, and a mission to reach audiences with a consciously determined relevance to their interests and point of view. At their best, these exhibitions have served their purpose well. They provide a powerful and useful framework for accessibility to important historical narratives and the people, events, artifacts, and stories that contribute to them.

But something has been lost in this process of professionalization, and Tammy Gordon provides us with some important insights as to why. Reading her manuscript, I was reminded of my visits to Knott's Berry Farm in the 1950s when I was growing up in Southern California. In addition to the hokey simulated gun battles and train robberies, there was a small, crude diorama of the trials and tribulations of the Knott ancestors as they traveled west. The spoken narrative was so personal and intimate that it was impossible not to be drawn into the Knotts' story. The script was obviously written by a member of the family and made up in intensity what it may have lacked in accuracy. In my young mind there was no question as to the story's authenticity—even if it might not have been completely true. I can still remember the setting, the scene, and the story almost word for word. I can also remember how it stimulated conversations in our family about family life in the past, the nature of hardship, and similar topics.

Professional historians and curators will of course object to the way that such presentations distort, fabricate, or in other ways use history and its artifacts for private purposes—and they should. But our concerns as historians and curators should not blind us to the many forms that a personal passion and involvement with the past can take. While we may criticize the lack of academic rigor in such presentations, we need to remember how much we depend on the latest trends in historical scholarship to inform our own work, and how quickly those trends change.

The exhibitions that Tammy Gordon focuses on in *Private History in Public* are just as invested in preserving and interpreting the past as those of the professionalized historical organization, but they do it in different way. Whether or not one agrees with Gordon's suggested typology of exhibitions, her focus on the importance of personality and intimacy, and their role in creating a conversation between the exhibition's creator and its audience, is important. The traditional curator gets his or her authority from scholarship; a community or entrepreneurial curator gets that same authority not only from research, but by the inclusion of a personal sense of lived experience and tradition and through identification with a particular community, business, or locale. Curating these exhibitions becomes an act of personal possession and creation, a way of engaging the world, possessing it, and making one's mark on it.

It is worthy of note that many of the best works of historical engagement recognize the importance of this intimacy and sense of personal story. The very best recent history books combine the interpretive perspective of the historian with the personal and particular perspective of the participant. The History Channel has long recognized that biography is a powerful lens from which to view the past and a good entry point into it. The best recent historical documentaries have strongly capitalized on personal stories and witnesses, usually caught on-camera, as an integral part of the interpretation of events. Ken Burns's documentary series on World War II is a supreme example of this, focusing almost exclusively on the war from the personal perspectives of participants. Yet by placing such weight on personal experience, Burns's World War II series loses the broader viewpoint and perspective of the historian. It has been rightly criticized for privatizing the experience of the war, "letting feelings eclipse history" in the words of *New York Times* critic Edward Rothstein.

Finding the right balance between the broadly historical and the personal and intimate is something that each individual history museum and history exhibition must determine for itself, according to its own organizational mission. We still very much need the academically based and institutionally produced history exhibitions that are so important in helping shape a public and accessible historical framework for seeing the world. A universe made up of history museums that all look like those described in *Private History in Public* would deprive us of important exhibitions with the professional historical and curatorial perspective that we have come to expect from major history museums.

Yet to paraphrase, history is too important to be left to the historians. One of the great strengths of the American museum movement has been its diversity. The types of exhibitions that are the focus of this book give a richness and variety to the history museum field. The fact that community-based, entrepreneurial, and vernacular exhibitions exist is a wonderful affirmation of the importance of the past in people's lives. If someone takes the time to look at his or her own work, or business, or life and put it into a historical context and is willing to share it, however personal and private, we are all the beneficiaries.

The exhibition genres that Tammy Gordon explores in this study clearly are of interest and value not only to their creators, but to others as well. They are both private and public. Simple observation reveals that they encourage conversation and dialogue about a great range of historical topics. Those of us who are professionals in the history field need to expand the boundaries of our own thinking so that we can better understand and engage with such exhibitions and those who create them. They are an integral part of our world.

Harold Skramstad
President
Henry Ford Museum & Greenfield Village

Acknowledgments

In addition to being a great joy, this research was challenging, and so was trying to explain it. Because of this, I asked for all kinds of help—help with funding, caring for children, writing, traveling, thinking—and I am lucky to be around people willing to assist.

My partner, Chris Gordon, is a road-tripper extraordinaire as well as a great educator. His support was invaluable and his insights were wry, witty, sometimes warped, but mostly dead-on. I am extremely lucky he is my fellow traveler. My children Josefina and Max Gordon accompanied me to museums, patiently waited for my return from research trips, and provided unique questions (trying to answer those inquiries so crucial to being six years old—"Do you love *all* old junk?"—helped me to articulate a number of points). As with most things, they made this process more meaningful and more fun. My parents Robert and Pat Stone made sure my children were happy and busy during those weeks I flew about the country, and knowing they were so well cared for allowed me to focus closely on my topic at key moments during the research process. They supported my studies in innumerable ways.

My years at the Michigan State University Museum, first as an exhibits assistant and then as assistant curator of exhibits, shaped my development as a professional and much of my thinking about the exhibition medium itself. Juan Alvarez, fantastic mentor and creative thinker, is the one to whom I owe the greatest thanks. His Room 7 graduates, including me, are amazingly lucky for the chance to work with him. Julie Avery, Kris Morrissey, and Ray Silverman inspired me to rise to the challenges of museum work and to never stop analyzing the processes of curation and communication. Gary Hoppenstand and Doug Noverr of the American Studies Program at

Michigan State University helped me to develop the skills and temperament necessary for attempting to understand the functions of popular culture in American society.

My colleagues and students in the History Department at the University of North Carolina, Wilmington have been crucial to the growth of this project. Students in my graduate seminars in museum education and museum exhibition forced me to sharpen my thinking about the relationships between curators and visitors. Will Moore, Director of Public History, has been a great friend and valued colleague, and his dedication to the ideals of public history are an inspiration. Lisa Pollard, Paul Townend, and Lynn Mollenaeur provided critical readings of those early, fairly deformed, and probably painful rough drafts. This book is better for their having read its first versions, particularly sections informed by a more global perspective. Sue McCaffray has been a wise and patient mentor, and helped me make the transition from museum to classroom. I am grateful to Yixin Chen for translating visitor surveys. The University of North Carolina, Wilmington also provided travel funding in the form of a Faculty Summer Research Initiative Grant and a Moseley Fund for Faculty Scholarship.

I am indebted to friends who shared their guest rooms, couches, and ideas for places to visit. Dawn and Todd Comer understood without question the appeal of this project, and took us to fantastic museums. I value greatly the intellectual and spiritual camaraderie I share with Dawn Comer, and the description of sites in this book are better because of her input. Maria Quinlan-Leiby and Susan Stein-Roggenbuck helped me formulate my original idea to study exhibition outside of museums, and they have been cherished friends. Anneli Saarvirita-Brazier, Mary Gordon, Niki and Eric Kirby, and Deb Pugh provided me with lodging and so allowed me to travel to more places.

The skills and professionalism of Jack Meinhardt, Marissa Parks and Karen Ackermann of Alta Mira Press are much appreciated.

People across the country who save historical objects and photos and then share them with strangers deserve my sincerest thanks. They took extra time to talk with me, give tours, tell stories, assist me with photos, and make me welcome. In particular, Rosemary Devinney of the Shoshone-Bannock Tribal Museum and Jim Anderson of the Olde Mill House Printing Museum taught me a great deal about museums, people, and life. They were generous with their time and knowledge and I consider myself fortunate to have learned from them. James DeCaire of Da Yoopers Tourist Trap and James Murphy of Murphy's Bleachers taught me how differently visitors see artifacts outside the museum setting. Museum visitors and bar patrons alike generously gave of their time and insights when asked for interviews. I am grateful for their honesty and offers of beer. I am likewise grateful for the journalists and bloggers who published accounts and photos of their visits to exhibits. You were perceptive visitors; thank you for that. My gratitude would not be complete without thanking those museums who conducted surveys for this study: Theo Dasbach's Rock and Roll and Blues Museum, the Smith Island Museum, Fort Fisher State Historic Site, Camp Van Dorn World War II Museum, the Great Plains Welsh Heritage Center, Schmidt House Museum, Moores Creek National Battlefield, and the McAllister House Museum. Your professionalism allowed this method to expand. Finally, I wish to thank people who run small museums for all your efforts to inspire visitors with the desire to learn history's lessons. Our understanding of history would be less nuanced—and in some cases less loud, gross, or strange—without you. Thank you.

1

Historical Display, Commerce, and Community

In August of 2004, I visited Da Yoopers Tourist Trap and Museum in Ish-peming, a small town in Michigan's Upper Peninsula. "Yooper" is a term used to describe residents of the U.P., a region on the southern Lake Su-perior shore known for its harsh weather and hardy population.[1] Da Trap was created by "Head Guy" Jim DeCaire and his musical group Da Yoopers, well known for their raucous performances and humorous depictions of life and culture in this remote region. Their single "Second Week of Deer Camp" is beloved by hunters across the nation. "Rusty Chevrolet" is like-wise a December favorite, a Christmas tune revolving around the trials of driving a clunker car. The gift shop and museum take a similarly irreverent approach to their topics. Visitors get to see dioramas of deer camp, with the roles of men and deer entirely inverted as the men hang upside down on the "man pole" while the deer sit in camp playing cards. Visitors can also examine the "ancient Yooper weather rock" (if rock is wet, it is raining . . .) and the world's largest operating chain saw. They can get a view of it all from the lower seat of a double-decker outhouse: Da Yooper 2-holer.

Amidst all the toilet humor, regional puns, and other fantastic silliness, however, is something much more complicated. Da Yoopers has collected material evidence of the local population's ability to adapt to harsh eco-nomic and weather conditions and displayed it with labels titled "Yooper Innovation." While some of these objects are elaborate material representa-tions of tall tales—like the 1937 iron bike race that pitted copper miners and iron miners in a race to see who was toughest—others are reasonable and verifiable historical representations of local adaptability. Homemade sleds and snowmobiles, winter outerwear and skis, snow scoops and snow plows, and the snowmachine and scooter interpreted with this label:

> Da Marvin Specials
> Homemade snowmachine and 1947 Cushman scooter with interchangeable 9½ h.p. cycle, air-cooled engine.
> Marvin is a lot like most Yooper guys in our area. Our mothers taught us at an early age to be thrifty and don't waste our hard earned money on toys. If you want a snow machine or motor bike, build your own. Marvin rode his snow machine in the winter and in da spring he changed da motor to da scooter and rode all summer. Pretty cool, hey! Built by Marvin Ruspakka, Humboldt, MI, 1961.

The idea of Marvin Ruspakka making his snowmachine in 1961 with scrap lumber, metal, and what could only have been the top part of an Eames chair knock-off, and his switching the engine seasonally to his late-forties scooter was enough to make a Yooper proud and an outsider envious of this heritage of cleverness. The fact the machines are fitted with dummies made of old clothes and Halloween masks of Bill and Hillary Clinton reflects the spirit of the object rather than detracts from the message of innovation and adaptability: the curators, in making the exhibits, used what they had. The Yooper Innovation objects assert rather stringently that local men have a history of cleverness, that their historically difficult economic conditions were opportunities for experiment, not impediments to thought or action. They even assert cultural superiority over the more privileged. Da Marvin Specials label is typical in that the curatorial voice is hardly third person: it reflects an individualized voice of someone telling his own history, not the history of others.

Another aspect of Da Yoopers Tourist Trap and Museum stood out to me: visitor behavior that indicated a deep level of engagement with the exhibit's themes. On this particular August day, which was "typical" in that the temperature barely touched 50 degrees by mid-afternoon and the drizzle swirled about sideways, visitors slowly worked their way through the outdoor exhibits. They pointed at objects regularly, talked about them with one another, and even read labels aloud to one another, all indicators of engaged visitor behavior according to the latest thinking in visitor studies. As they hunched in the wind over small Styrofoam cups of coffee, visitors were taking their time and enthusiastically enjoying themselves and the topic.

At that time I was working as an exhibits developer at a university museum and had even created displays about the Upper Peninsula, so I had to wonder why visitors to our exhibits—developed according to professional standards—only rarely demonstrated the kind of enthusiasm they showed so consistently when looking at Yooper Innovation objects. It would have

Figure 1.1. Human models driving Da Marvin Specials (note the Bill and Hillary Clinton masks). (Da Yoopers Tourist Trap, Ishpeming, Michigan, 2004. Photo by author.)

been easy to look down my professional exhibit-developer's nose at the
shabby labels, the obvious lack of conservation techniques, and the trails
that could not have begun to meet Americans with Disabilities Act-inspired
guidelines. But these visitors, these objects that attested to a unique history
and culture, these labels that seemed so friendly (and a personal distaste for
looking down my nose at anything) led me instead to investigate the exhibits rarely acknowledged by our scholarship in museum studies and public
history: those in small community museums, restaurants, bars, beauty
shops, and even in people's homes. Da Yoopers Tourist Trap and Museum
was the silliest, most irreverent museum I would encounter in the years of
this investigation, but it had one thing in common with scores of others
around the country: Americans use small community museums and other
settings of daily life to create exhibits that tell a history from an *individualized perspective*. Historical curation is much, much more than a professional
practice. It is a social one, a practice in which strangers discuss their own
views of the past with one another.

This book is about history exhibits like Yooper Innovation that complicate the public/private dichotomy, exhibits that promote individualized perspectives to strangers and cement ties between relatives, friends,
colleagues, and community members. Exhibits in small museums attract
people to converse about community, national, or international issues in
the context of local history. At the same time, so can displays of artifacts
in community centers, bars, restaurants, shops, beauty parlors, and even
plumbing supply houses. Historic objects serve to explain communities,
families, and individuals to outsiders and tie insiders together around a
shared narrative of historical experience. Sometimes, direct political action
emerges from the spaces occupied by displays of historic objects. More
often, the act of asserting one's historical narrative is in itself political, especially if one holds ideas of history that run counter to dominant narratives.
For these reasons, private history exhibits—those that reflect individualized
perspectives on history—need our attention.

Traditionally, scholars writing on historical exhibition have focused on
highly professionalized exhibits in large, publicly funded museums.[2] This
has left the majority of historical exhibits—and their techniques, functions,
and social roles—regrettably understudied. Scholarly neglect of exhibits
in small museums, nontraditional museums, and in non-museum settings leads to conclusions about exhibition practice that do not reflect
the majority of visitor interaction with historical exhibits. Ultimately, this
neglect of the less formal exhibition has a negative effect on all museums,
for visitors do not discriminate among exhibit types as much as scholars
have chosen to do. Visitors seek out a variety of exhibits, not just the highly
professionalized, nationally visible ones. Their ideas about museums are
shaped by a diversity of exhibits, but scholarly ideas about exhibits have

reflected primarily one type. Museums have become ubiquitous. Towns too small for grocery stores have historical museums. As Americans continue to design their public spaces—in the Disneyland tradition—according to theme on both large and small scales,[3] it seems every third restaurant meal is accompanied by material evidence of the past. While the global economy supposedly homogenizes cultural difference, local economies step up to assert their uniqueness through the exhibition medium. These social and economic trends point to a need to rework our ideas to come to terms with the *full range* of historical exhibition practices in the United States, not just the highly professionalized ones. Because of the increase in the past's marketability and the attendant rise in historical exhibitions in non-museum settings, analysis restricted to the publicly funded, large museum model no longer will do as the primary source for scholarship in museum studies.

The lack of analysis of smaller, individualized history exhibits also means we are missing crucial insights into the role of private history in the shaping of democracy and the ways in which communities promote their sovereignty. In small community museums, truck stops, restaurants, bars, barbershops, schools, and churches, people create displays to tell the neglected histories that matter to them. Much of this history is personal: family history, community history, the history of one's trade, or the history of something considered less than genteel. It is often history based on feelings, beliefs, and memory. Roy Rosenzweig and David Thelen's 1998 groundbreaking study *The Presence of the Past: Popular Uses of History in American Life* shows that Americans tend to focus on the "intimate past," history as it relates to individuals and their families. They are less likely to feel connected to the past that so fascinates professional historians, like events of national importance, the change over time of whole societies, and the political affairs of nation-states. These exhibits' intimate spaces and hybrid epistemologies break down the traditional hierarchies between curators and visitors. Because of this, the small, often nonprofessionalized history exhibit is the medium through which individuals connect their "private histories" to those of other individuals. These spaces lend themselves well to cross-group interaction, one of the most important characteristics of a civil society. Distrustful of overproduced messages from the media or other large institutions in American life, the creators and users of these displays see these exhibitions as ways of bringing individuals together around ideas about the past. They provide spaces in which strangers meet to talk about the past and its applicability to present society. Such conversations are the foundation of democratic action and have the potential to change social practices and even policy. The exhibits described in this book demonstrate that more is at stake than a fun visit to a roadside attraction; these exhibits are the sites of cross-class, cross-ethnic, cross-culture conversations that can ultimately lead to social and economic changes.

This does not mean that visitors accept private history interpretations as the "Truth," nor is it the point of this book to validate historical inaccuracies where they appear in exhibits. Rather, it is to show the circumstances that produce expressions of individual perspectives through the exhibition medium and to assert that visitors are quite capable of seeing private history exhibits as representing perspective. This phenomenon does not threaten or compete with the traditional authority of professionalized, academic exhibits in large museums. Private history exhibits do not replace academic ones; they supplement them or provide alternate viewpoints. Because visitors pay attention to private history exhibits, so should scholars of history and museum studies.

The term "private" as used in this book refers to historical information that, up until about thirty years ago, circulated within relatively small social groups like families, colleagues, regular patrons of a particular establishment, or community members. For a number of reasons but principally the growth of electronic media, knowledge thought private in earlier periods has made its way into public discourse through television talk shows starting in the 1970s to today's proliferation of blogs and other Web 2.0 tools like Facebook and YouTube. Historical knowledge has followed the openness trend that has characterized other sorts of information in this period. As the primary mechanism of communication about material history, the exhibition medium allowed users to present history with their own belongings. As will be discussed later in chapter 5, this trend toward publicizing private information accompanied the growth of a leisure economy that privileged experience as much as product. The heightened public dialogue on the meaning of individual and group identity was the third enabling factor for private history exhibits in the United States.

The term "public" has received its share of attention in this same period, drawing on scholarly and popular debates that have their roots in the Enlightenment. Over the twentieth century, writers both in- and outside academia debated the role of the public in government, the individual's role in public life, the survival of the "public sphere" in the age of mass communication.[4] This book uses the term "public" as an adjective to describe spaces to which anyone is welcome, at least in the legal sense. Some of the spaces in which private history exhibits appear do fall into a rather liminal area between heavily restricted space and open-access space. Some exhibits emphasize the insider voice so heavily that outsiders are merely tolerated, as is the case of Tony Polito's Barber Shop and Military Museum, where patrons prefer a masculine environment. A female visitor could of course legally access the museum, but she would hardly face a hearty welcome, especially, according to Tony Polito, if she happened to be a Hillary Clinton supporter.[5] The "publicness" of a space is always open to debate, but in the case of the exhibits presented in this book, "public" refers to the fact they are made for and used by people not always personally known to the curator. Private history exhibits are meant to cement heritage ties among group members and explain that heritage—from the insider perspective—to outsiders.

Nontraditional history exhibits present some interesting methodological challenges. They cannot be assessed simply in terms of historiography because their epistemologies are diverse. Often blending ideas from history, the oral tradition, folklore, popular culture, and personal preference, they represent an utterance that is culturally, economically, and politically situated in the present. To further complicate (and enhance) the investigation of exhibition, the visitors of these exhibits bring their own knowledge base and motivations to their understanding of the themes. This book is ethnographic in that it is a study of a social setting. As such, it employs methods from the fields of visitor studies and oral history. In seeking to understand the social, cultural, and economic circumstances that led to private history exhibits in their contemporary forms, this book is also historical.

In her classic work on exhibit development, *Planning for People in Museum Exhibitions*, Kathleen McLean rightly states that exhibitions are "containers for human activity."[6] Like other containers, the ones so thoroughly examined by archaeologists and art historians, exhibitions reveal a great deal about the societies that made and used them. While the objects in exhibits usually take center stage in scholarly examinations, the flow of meaning—including meaning created by visitors—through the physical space of the exhibit is less examined. Because it looks at knowledge flow between curator and visitor and among visitors in a defined physical space, this book could also be called a material culture study. It examines the life and meanings of an object: the exhibit. Even more specifically, this study employs Prownian analysis. Art history scholar Jules David Prown emphasizes the role of the senses in material culture analysis. He asserts that "by undertaking cultural interpretation through artifacts, we engage the other culture in the first instance not with our minds, the seat of our cultural biases, but with our senses."[7] The "culture" represented by this book is not the culture of the host museum but the culture of exhibits—the social cues, conventions, artistry, rituals, and communication techniques that make up the culture of exhibit creation and visitation. While I couldn't feasibly have used my senses in every exhibit mentioned in this book, I did visit many of them, which allowed me to approach them in Prownian fashion. This approach forced me to consider some rather unusual themes in some rather unusual things. I pondered the real strangeness of death as I stared way too long at the thick blond moustache of the corpse of a cowboy on display at Ye Olde Curiosity Shop in Seattle, Washington. At a seventies display in a Michigan thrift shop, I wondered at the human desire for color as I felt the alien-skin texture of a polyester pantsuit and concluded the color saturation made its tactile eeriness worthwhile. It showed me how Viking soup can smell like friendship and how seeing beaded moccasins can make some people cry over their ancestors' persecutions of others. In short, I became a heavily engaged museum visitor, for whom everyone—visitors, curators, and researchers like me—and everything—objects, text, dirty fingerprints on warm Plexiglas—was part of the meaning of the exhibition. This method, while it certainly could not provide me with a complete understanding of the function of historical display, added the nuances to the conclusions emerging out of more traditional methods.

Before we can understand exactly how history exhibits in small museums and non-museum settings are sites of dialogue, we must fully engage a definition of the exhibition medium. One of the reasons scholars may have avoided the small museum and exhibits in non-museum settings is that some of them emerge from the "dime museum" tradition of emphasizing the exotic or scandalous. It is true that some of the interpretation in roadside museums would never fulfill the demands of academic historical method: objectivity, multiple perspectives, and rigorous analysis. Many others, however, could. It is important, however, to study how knowledge is constructed, or *situated* (according to Donna Haraway's terminology[8]). We must understand these exhibitions through their own logic, from their role in the community, their own individualized perspectives, whether supported by historiography or not. Dixie Evans, who ran the Strippers Hall of Fame in Helendale, California, put it best when she defended her museum: "We're trying to protect our past. Whether people approved or disapproved, we existed."[9] Such efforts to manage the story of one's past are significant enough to warrant the attention of scholars.

Public history scholarship provides some background on the exhibition as a cultural product developed collaboratively among professionals, academics, and communities. As an academic field, public history developed in distinction to "academic history," or history produced for an academic readership. Public history scholars have criticized "traditional" history for its elitism, but in terms of producing scholarship on exhibition, its focus has largely been on professionalized—even elite—museums. The field's founders took inspiration from an academic job crisis and from experience with formally trained historians working in government, archives, museums, and libraries.[10] In recounting the developmental years of public history as an academic field, professor and one of the founders of *The Public Historian,* G. Wesley Johnson notes that while public history seems to require a good measure of explanation to an academic audience, the public fully understands the relevance of trained historians engaged in work outside academe. He writes that the phenomenon "suggested to me that indeed public history was a concept whose time had come, and the public at large was one step ahead of the historians in accepting it. They knew they needed help."[11] Other scholars have supported his observation, and some—notably Michael Frisch in *Shared Authority: Essays on the Craft and Meaning of Oral and Public History*—have theorized the concept.[12] While public history provides significant understanding of relationships between history curators (usually in larger professionalized museums) and the public, it has not provided a framework for understanding diverse exhibition practices. Public history scholars are academicians training students for professional settings, and the focus on professionalized museums emerges from this; to fully understand museum exhibition, however, we need to broaden the scope of study.[13]

Museum studies scholars—particularly those using anthropological or sociological methods—provide additional insight into the relationships between exhibition creators and exhibition users. Visitor studies in particular have paralleled public history's interest in the role of the public in the development of museum function and programming. Unlike public historians, museum studies scholars examine exhibits on subject matter beyond history. Using methods from education and sociology, scholars in visitor studies have been a major force transforming the museum's role from a top-down, authoritative institution to one that includes multiple voices and recognizes the necessity and value of community input. Museum professionals produced a number of guidelines that help those in the field include and engage visitors and communities. Professionals in history museums built on methods developed for science museums and began to integrate community groups into their development process.[14] Scholarship on the relationships between museums and their publics, however, employs primarily a large museum model.

Some anthropologists studying museums have departed from the practice of privileging the large, professionalized museum. Christina Kreps uses Nick Stanley's concept of "indigenous curation" to break down the assumption that contemporary professionalized museum methods—those based on international knowledge derived from scientific and academic traditions—are not always helpful in making museums responsive to community needs.[15] She studies museums from Indonesia, the Netherlands, and the United States to assert the diversity of valid museum practices. The dichotomy, however, between "professionalized" and "indigenous" is problematic. A more useful framework for studying exhibition must recognize that *all* curation is responsive to the needs of a defined community, whether local or global, formally educated or not. This means studying exhibitions according to their epistemologies, looking at each exhibit's source of knowledge and purpose for delivering it. Such an approach problematizes the uneven relationships between curator and visitor, between the museum and the public.

Museum studies and public history literatures are alike in their conceptions of the role of the public, that curators "share" their authority with
the public. The willingness of the public to participate in both museum
work and historical inquiry is more than simple generosity or need of
professional help, however. In the case of museum exhibits, the public's
willingness and ability to participate in exhibition development comes in
large part from the fact that people encounter history exhibits in the spaces
of their daily lives. Exhibition is a medium with which Americans are quite
familiar. Public engagement in exhibits at large museums is not at all sur-
prising; people know how to "share authority" in exhibits because they are
already engaged in practices similar to professional ones.[16]

Literature in tourism studies has broadened the study of historical
exhibition and illuminated ways in which museum behavior operates in
the larger culture and the socioeconomic trends that have made local heritage highly marketable.[17] Tony Bennett makes the historical connection
between museums and other public leisure activities like amusement
resorts, midways, and department stores. He traces the history of the
museum as an institution that "provided a mechanism for the transformation of the crowd into an ordered and, ideally, self-regulating public,"
an effect shared by other places of organized leisure and consumption.
This "exhibitionary complex" allows for a reevaluation of material culture and heritage, resulting in public (professional) administration of
heritage and scientific resources.[18] Bella Dicks provides a description of
"contemporary visitability," the phenomenon in which public space has
a museal function. Contemporary public spaces are planned for maxi-
mum viewing pleasure, scripted with signs both textual and visual that
traditionally have been the markers of meaning for museum exhibitions
since the formation of the public museum. These scripts are aimed at attracting tourist dollars. Dicks provides new understanding of heritage: "If
we think of heritage as *history made visitable* we can avoid falling into un-
productive debates over truth v. distortion. What this means is that heritage is produced within the cultural economy of visitability, in which the
object is to attract as many visitors as practicable to the intended site, and
to communicate with them in meaningful terms."[19] Dicks's formulation
brings earlier work on tourism and ethnographic display together with
historical display to assert the interconnectedness among globalization,
heritage, and consumerism. The argument points to a need for a revised
typology of historical exhibition, one that recognizes the proliferation
and diversity of historical display and the integration of museum visitor
behavior into the public spaces of everyday life.

"Toward a New Typology of Historical Exhibition in the United States,"
the second chapter in this book, calls for a revision of the current vocabulary of museum exhibition types. Drawing on interviews with visitors and

curators and documentation of exhibitions, this chapter provides the foundation for studying public dialogue in exhibitions I term:

- *Community*, usually called "local history," in which curators with a heavy investment in the topic through descent or personal experience, tell the history of their specific place or community from their own perspective.
- *Entrepreneurial*, in which practitioners of a trade or craft explain its history to perpetuate artisanal cultures and traditions and in so doing imitate the methods and functions of small business.
- *Vernacular*, which occurs in non-museum spaces and may or may not relate thematically to its location. This type makes consumption an act of community identification.

These types are distinct from *Academic Exhibition*, conducted by professionals using academic research methods, and *Corporate Exhibition*, which uses professional exhibition techniques and blends academic research with marketing needs.

"Community Exhibition: History, Identity, and Dialogue," the third chapter, draws on visitor evaluation research as well as interviews with curators to examine the role of community-based identity in public dialogue about the past. This chapter demonstrates that visitors are highly aware of a museum's institutional perspective and see the small museum as representative of community. Curators, as the case study on The Shoshone-Bannock Tribal Museum demonstrates, understand that what visitors learn affects policy governing the community and—in this case—ultimately informs tribal sovereignty. Examples from other community history museums demonstrate similar processes, in which local communities use the exhibition medium to assert independence from and interaction with a nationalized or globalized culture and economy.

"Entrepreneurial Exhibition: Historical Display and the Small Business Tradition," chapter 4, looks at exhibits made by those in a particular job, trade, craft, or profession. Exhibits made by firefighters, printers, nurses, educators, police officers, and even, in one case, freak-show workers, demonstrate attempts by workers to criticize some of the hierarchies of American society, particularly those based on class. At the same time, they validate the possibility of attaining the American Dream, albeit in moral and not economic terms. Often modeled spatially on the small business, these exhibits encourage personal connections among individuals. Face-to-face conversation is the single most important interpretive technique in these exhibits, demonstrating the opportunities smaller exhibits have for facilitating the cross-race, cross-language, and cross-class connections that are so important to the survival of American democracy.

Chapter 5, "Vernacular Exhibition and the Business of History," shows that visitors and curators do not separate the educational function of exhibitions from the commercial function of the setting. In fact, experiencing artifacts in the business setting makes them feel more tied to a particular community. The case study on Murphy's Bleachers, a museum bar on Chicago Cubs history in Wrigleyville, shows that users tailor their ideas about history to the spaces where that history is told. Demographically similar to National Museum of American History visitors, patrons at Murphy's see history not a something to be learned (as they did at NMAH) but something to be experienced in the present as living tradition. Documentation from other exhibits in barbershops, restaurants, and other settings reveal similar connections. Communities formed of people who do not necessarily live together—like the community of Cubs fans validated by the history presented in Murphy's Bleachers—can end up claiming spaces, resources, and indeed the power to influence policy. Indeed, Murphy's became a center of community action on issues relating to bleacher expansion and the neighborhood's legal relationship to the Cubs franchise.

Chapter 6, "Local History, Global Economy: The Functions of History Exhibits in the Settings of Everyday Life," examines ways in which community, entrepreneurial, and vernacular exhibitions emerge from the economic changes of the past thirty years: the rise in tourism, the increasing demand for "experience commodities" consumed in themed environments, and the burgeoning market niche of local history in a global economy that has supposedly homogenized culture. Interviews with visitors indicate that the history exhibit serves a range of needs, such as opportunities for meaningful conversations with strangers and connections to community. Such phenomena demonstrate that history exhibits in small museums and in non-museum settings have important roles in cross-regional, interethnic, and international dialogue on heritage and culture.

This book is organized by type of exhibition and chronologically by each type's emergence. Historical exhibition in the United States emerged and changed during periods of intense growth in the leisure economy, but also solidified in its present forms during periods in which public dialogue on identity amplified. Community exhibition has its roots in nationalism, and appeared earliest. Entrepreneurial exhibition drew on this tradition but modified it to assert the primacy of work in individual and collective identities. Vernacular exhibition emerged latest, as themed environments became an integral part of the experience economy of the later twentieth century. Despite their differences, community, entrepreneurial, and vernacular exhibitions are alike in that they rely heavily on face-to-face conversation, experiential knowledge, and individualized perspectives. They share the same goal of inviting visitors into histories that are more private than the dominant national narratives. They differ, however, in their relationship to commerce, in their level of participation in the market economy. Community exhibits are more aloof from market exigencies, although they are part of the movement in which cultural and entertainment venues drive local economies. They appear in stand-alone museums, and are usually funded by governments or visitors. Entrepreneurial exhibits are more likely to be dependent on businesses or curators' own funds; whatever the funding source, however, the exhibit imitates the logic and function of small business. Vernacular exhibits appear in the same space and are dependent upon a business. They are usually part of the business's function. This organization is more than just an academic exercise. An exhibit's relationship to commerce and market heavily informs visitor behavior and perceptions of history. While they may have similar artifacts, sports exhibits in museums and in bars (for example) will produce different reactions in visitors. People go to museums to *learn* history; people go to bars with artifacts to *feel a part* of history. In addition, the dominant theme in each exhibit type corresponds to areas of visitors' identities. Community exhibits connect to visitors because visitors themselves are members of place-based communities. Entrepreneurial exhibits rely on visitors seeing themselves as workers or future workers. Vernacular exhibits imply that because visitors consume goods and services in the exhibit setting, they are a part of the community depicted. As consumers, they are managed by market segmentation, partly through the exhibit; however, visitors and curators communicate in ways that go beyond the producer/consumer dynamic, making the site of the vernacular exhibit a center of more traditional community life.

Within one site, a museum may have all three types or characteristics of all three types, each occurring in spaces whose function is determined by its relationship to commerce. Even though these exhibits are heavily influenced by capitalism, they are also significant to the function of democracy, for they encourage individuals' participation in the direction of their communities. Individuals who make history exhibits express publicly their personal ideas about community issues, and sometimes national or international ones. This leads to dialogue and sometimes even political action. Other times the act of self-definition alone is a political act. Ordered by consumer behavior and the exigencies of a market economy, exhibitions abound between the museum bar and the professionalized exhibition. It is the goal of this book to understand how they function to negotiate boundaries and create dialogue.

2

Toward a New Typology of Historical Exhibition in the United States

Private history exhibits share an approach to curatorial voice. The chosen objects are not just "artifacts" but are instead a curator's *belongings*. The term *artifact* is scientific, connoting a representative sample or an exceptional example of a type. By definition, artifacts held in the public trust by institutions are not representations of a curator's identity. Belongings, on the other hand, are the material evidence of one's identity. They are what is left from one's ancestors or they reflect more recent personal tastes and hobbies: collections of lunch boxes, comic books, sports memorabilia, or antiques. When displayed, one's belongings are interpreted by the individual to whom they belong. Artifacts, by contrast, are interpreted with a curatorial voice that represents an institution engaged in more traditional academic research. While multiple perspectives are represented, the curatorial voice is not individualized. Exhibition, as a medium used to explain both artifacts and belongings, lends itself to a diversity of forms and is hence employed in a number of settings by practitioners with multiple ideas on its purpose and function.

To sort out the many types of exhibitions and understand the conditions that produce private history exhibits, we need to understand exhibits according to their own variables: institutional framework and gallery techniques. The institutional framework of the exhibition includes the exhibit's physical setting, its knowledge sources, its purpose, staff training, and funding. These inform another set of variables more closely related to the gallery setting: exhibition design and resources, collections care, and visitor expectations. These variables exist in combinations that describe most types of historical exhibition: academic, corporate, community, entrepreneurial, and vernacular. Of course, individual exhibitions are more complicated than the categories set up here, and many have characteristics of two or more categories. However, without a solid vocabulary of museal display types, scholars make assumptions about the practice of exhibition based on only one type: that of the large, publicly funded, professionalized museum.

Academic exhibition, formed on principles of academic and market research, receives the most public scrutiny and scholarly attention. Audience is broadly conceived and carefully studied through rounds of front-end, formative, and summative evaluation. While exhibits may be funded with soft money, the institution's funding is comparatively stable (if this can be said of any public historical museum in the United States) and usually funded in large part by government or corporate donors. Museums with exhibits of this type bring together diverse viewpoints and serve diverse user groups. The visitor gaze is highly managed within the gallery, using commercial design styles and materials and high-end technology. The collections have equal—or even less—visual weight than constructed elements.

Many of the exhibits studied in the classic work on exhibit development, *Ideas and Images: Developing Interpretive History Exhibits*, are academic exhibits: "From Victory to Freedom: Afro-American Life in the Fifties," "The Way to Independence: Memories of a Hidatsa Indian Family, 1840–1920," and "Fit For America: Health, Fitness, Sport, and American Society, 1830–1940." Scholars have also documented the narratives, development processes, and controversies associated with academic exhibitions, often faulting them for not being critical enough of subject matter, such as Mike Wallace's discussion of Ellis Island exhibits, Steven C. Dubin's work on *The West as America* and the now infamous *Enola Gay* interpretive plan, or Richard Handler and Eric Gable's ethnographic study of Colonial Williamsburg.[1]

Academic exhibits use academic research methods and conventions to mediate among diverse viewpoints. Such is the case with *The Dead Sea Scrolls*, a 2003 exhibition at the Grand Rapids Public Museum, the largest museum in western Michigan. *The Dead Sea Scrolls* featured twelve fragments from the Dead Sea Scrolls on loan from the Israel Antiquities Authority and had broad participation from both community groups and scholars. Public programming was ambitious, including a public lecture series featuring an impressive list of scholars, an academic conference, performances, "Learning Lunches," and family workshops. One of the main themes of the exhibit was to de-sensationalize rumors that either Jews or Christians manipulated the processing of the scrolls to stabilize the validity of each religion. Exhibit text emphasized the common origins of the world's three monotheistic religions: "The Dead Sea Scrolls provide a window into an incredible time in history—the time when Judaism as we know it today was formed; the time when Christianity was born; and the time when the seeds of Islam were sown." Curator Ellen Middlebrook Herron wrote that "per-

Table 2.1. Exhibition Type and Institutional Framework Variables

Exhibition Type	Physical Setting	Knowledge Source	Purpose	Staff	Funding
Academic	Museum	Academic/international	Mediate among diverse viewpoints and promote broadly based public dialogue	Professionally trained in museology	Government, corporate, visitor revenue, endowments
Corporate	Stand-alone museum or company headquarters	Academic/market research	Marketing/public relations	Professionally trained	Corporate
Community	Museum	Hybrid: academic, experiential, oral tradition, religion	Ethnographic salvage; assert local control of heritage resources	Both professional and non-professional; volunteers	Smaller governmental entities like county, city, or tribe, private donations and visitor revenue, sometimes endowments
Entrepreneurial	Museum connected to a small business	Hybrid: primarily experiential, academic	Encourage survival of craft	Not professionally trained; volunteers	Dependent on small business and visitor revenue
Vernacular	Bar, restaurant, beauty parlor, or other retail or service setting	Hybrid: local, experiential, religion, oral tradition, popular culture	Create "atmosphere"; assert local control of heritage resources	Not professionally trained; volunteers	Dependent on small business or organization

Table 2.2. Exhibition Type and Gallery Setting Variables

Type	Exhibition Resources and Design	Collections Care	Visitor Expectations[1]
Academic	Pathways and visitor gaze highly managed by both 2D and 3D elements, commercial materials, built manipulatives	Controlled environment, specialized mounts, heavy security (cases, security screws); care informed by professional standards	Expect authoritative or dominant narratives to connect to experiences in formal education
Corporate	Pathways and visitor gaze highly managed by both 2D and 3D elements, commercial materials, heavily manipulative or immersive	Controlled environment, specialized mounts, heavy security (cases, security screws); care informed by professional standards	Expect company history and entertainment
Community	Artifacts and labels dominate, artifacts more accessible, simple manipulatives, varying degrees of pathway and gaze management; first person interpreters	Varying degrees of environmental control and mount specialization, care informed by a combination of professional standards and community culture and goals	Expect "local heritage," sometimes at odds with "what we learned in school"
Entrepreneurial	Main delivery is first-person, face-to-face, and conversational, demonstrations, some label text	Few environmental controls and few specialized mounts	Expect face-to-face conversation with a person having experiential knowledge of the topic; small business atmosphere
Vernacular	Primarily artifacts and photos with some labels	Environment controlled by business needs, low- to mid-level security (against theft), mounts not usually preservation-minded	Find artifacts appealing because it lends "atmosphere" or "authenticity" to their eating, drinking, retail or service experience

[1] This information is based on eighty-nine interviews with visitors at exhibits in these settings and published reports in visitor studies from the Smithsonian Office of Policy and Analysis and the National Park Service. These will be discussed in later chapters.

haps the true legacy of the Dead Sea Scrolls is their power to bring people together."[2] Such an approach is typical of academic exhibition: scholarship on the past to inform solutions to contemporary problems.

Academic exhibits often reflect the newest ideas in the museum studies field. *Teen Chicago* at the Chicago History Museum is a case study in best professional practices, and employed a technique often used by highly professionalized museums to share authority: multiple perspectives. This exhibit, however, went beyond diversity in interpretation and began development with a Teen Council composed of fifteen teens from across the

Figure 2.1. Interactive element from Teen Chicago. Academic and corporate exhibits rely heavily on constructed elements. (Chicago History Museum, 2004. Photo by author.)

city and surrounding suburbs. The museum employed these teens, trained them in museum practice and oral history methods, and provided research guidance. The council was integrated into every facet of exhibition development, resulting in a highly engaging exhibition. It employed multimedia presentations, digital and mechanical interactives, object-based interpretation, and a 2D design motif that bordered on graphic saturation. Members of the Teen Council and CHS professionals reported the exhibition development experience of *Teen Chicago* was transformative. The American Association of Museums gave its approval through an award in the Excellence in Exhibition Competition.[3]

While experimental in some ways, academic exhibits will regularly stress traditional historical subjects like the affairs of nation-states and change over time. The core exhibits at the Palace of the Governors in Santa Fe are a case in point. As part of the Museum of New Mexico system, the museum's mission is to educate visitors about the long and varied history of New Mexico, its tri-culturalism, and its role in international affairs. The building itself reflects this theme. Built in 1609–1610 by the Spanish, the Palace of the Governors was the seat of government through Spanish, Mexican, and American control. The core exhibits highlight state history with a governmental theme: an 1845 Mexican governor's office, Governor Bradford Prince's 1893 reception room, a portrait gallery, and cases on "The Spanish Frontier," "The Anglo Frontier," and period cases highlighting different phases of New Mexico as contested terrain. Timelines play a prominent visual and thematic role in exhibition.[4]

Academic exhibits are more likely to employ theoretical label text. *Without Sanctuary: Lynching Photography in America* at the Wright Museum of African American History in Detroit provides an example of this phenomenon. This exhibit displays photographs of people lynched in the United States between the latter half of the nineteenth century and 1981, Ku Klux Klan dress and jewelry, a quilt, a camera, recorded oral histories of lynchings, and numerous 2D artifacts. Conceptually sophisticated and self-aware, this exhibit asks visitors to pay close attention, as explained in the introductory text to the first section, *Lynching: A Somber Phenomenon*: "As you go through the exhibition, take time to read the labels. In a sense, they are the obituaries for the victims of a society that ignored the persecution of thousands of its citizens."[5] Section text is styled in academic prose. This section label, on metaphorical lynching, reflects the theoretical focus of many academic exhibits:

Lynching as Metaphor
    African Americans have for centuries been conscious of their image as an ethnic group. A negative collective image—popularized in stereotypes and circulated in mass media caricatures—reflected and reinforced society's misunderstanding, non-appreciation, intolerance and even hatred of blacks. Such xenophobia expressed by whites, and learned by other ethnic groups socialized into the "American way," served as a pretext for acts now characterized as "hate

crimes," especially lynching. In fact, it is indeed possible to speak of stereotypes, caricatures, and character assassinations as forms of metaphorical lynching. Devoid of physical carnage, the intergenerational psychosocial damage that may be inflicted on members of an entire ethnic group *via* metaphorical lynching is, nevertheless, a method of control to "keep them in their place."[6]

These examples demonstrate that academic exhibits differ from other museal displays in curatorial desire to mediate knowledge, the exhibit's role in encouraging dialogue on national issues, and reliance on academic research methods and, sometimes, language.

While the corporate exhibition shares some academic methods, its purpose is decidedly more connected to marketing a particular product or company. These exhibits explain the large company's success. Using professional development and materials, the corporate exhibit employs history as indirect advertising. Victor Danilov defines the corporate museum as "a corporate facility with tangible objects and/or exhibits, displayed in a museum-like setting, that communicates the history, operations, and/or interests of a company to employees, guests, customers, and/or the public."[7] Danilov summarizes the purposes of corporate museums, citing some in common with other types of museums, like being a repository of artifacts or serving the public. Corporate museums differ from others, however, in that they seek to "influence public opinion about the company and/or controversial issues" and to "serve as a showcase for the company's collections and/or products."[8] The History Factory, a company that develops and fabricates corporate historical exhibits, summed up the purpose of corporate exhibition: "A corporate museum or historical installation is the ultimate showcase of your organization's history and an amazing brand-building tool."[9]

Research on corporate exhibits is either from the fields of marketing or museum studies. Danilov's work documents corporate museums and serves as a resource for companies planning corporate exhibits.[10] Mark Rectanus provides a more critical approach not of corporate museums per se, but of corporate sponsorship of public museum exhibits, asserting that corporations have been using museums "as a public relations instrument" in the United States since the 1950s.[11] Except for the isolated exhibit review, there is virtually no scholarship on corporate exhibition techniques and how these might differ from those used by other types of museums.[12]

Exhibits in the Levi Strauss & Company Museum or the Wells Fargo History Museum are this type, which rely heavily on high-end constructed elements for visual impact. The quintessential corporate exhibits, however, are found at the World of Coca-Cola in Atlanta, Georgia. Ted Friedman described the interpretive approach:

Looming over all of the exhibitions at the *World of Coca-Cola* is the question of control: who owns Coca-Cola? Again and again the *World of Coca-Cola* impresses upon visitors that it is a "consumer's eye view," a cultural history of

Coca-Cola. But it is a strange kind of cultural history, told not from the bottom up, but from the top down. It tells its story exclusively through materials generated by the Coca-Cola Corporation. . . . And so while the *World of Coca-Cola* often claims that Coke belongs to everybody, it is engaged in a continual effort to circumscribe the way Coca-Cola is defined to include only corporate-originated communication.[13]

While there is some effort to connect Coke to broader themes in U.S. and world history, the effort is primarily to tell the story of market dominance and consumer loyalty: "the Coke story is told absolutely without tension or conflict—except insofar as rivals and pretenders are concerned."[14] Visitors can choose multimedia presentations, view a kinetic sculpture on bottling, visit a 1930s soda counter re-creation, or touch off a coke fountain by offering it a glass of ice. World of Coca-Cola presents a dazzling selection of exhibition and theme park technologies.[15]

The corporate exhibit presents scholars with interesting possibilities for visitor studies, given the complicated dynamics of marketing to a society oversaturated in advertising. Indeed, Margot Wallace's work on "museum branding" reflects a recent effort by museums to employ image management techniques previously associated with for-profits. This direction in museum studies has potential for revealing how visitors conceive of themselves as consumers of the educational experience and how this conception affects learning.[16]

The community exhibit is similar to the academic exhibit, but it usually differs in size, funding, and curatorial role vis-á-vis the community. The latter is the most striking feature of the community exhibition: it is produced by people who have close personal or ancestral ties to the topic being presented. They interpret the particular history because they or their parents/grandparents/ancestors lived it. These exhibits rely on blends of local and academic authority, and professional and nonprofessional staff. Funding is primarily from small governmental entities like a municipality, town, county, or tribe. From a standpoint of display style, the objects have more visual impact than the constructed elements, and the implied visitor is conceived of as one of two types: local or outsider. Visitors' motivations are to get "local heritage" rather than broad understandings of historic themes. Nick Stanley's concept of "indigenous curation" refers to curation practices by those who are both curator and subject and is an apt phrase for describing the curatorial approach in the community exhibit. The people creating the exhibit are its subject or are otherwise connected to the history they are telling. They are also usually very tied to place. Scholarship has focused on those exhibits that offer particularly skewed history, like the slavery exhibits documented by Jennifer Eichstedt and Stephen Small and the historic sites described by James Loewen.[17] Community exhibition does not necessarily equate with bad history, however, and the recent collection *Defining*

Figure 2.2.   Label on garden cart used to haul bodies by serial killer Belle Gunness. Community exhibits rely more on the impact of artifacts than on high-end signage and constructed elements. (LaPorte County Historical Society, LaPorte, Indiana. Photo by author.)

Memory: Local Museums and the Construction of History in America's Changing Communities used a theoretical framework from education to hypothesize how people learn in local history settings, even if practices in these museums are sometimes far from dominant professional exhibition practices.[18]

Indigenous curation, however, is about more than local history. Local history exhibits may be constructed by those outside the community. Community exhibits provide individualized perspectives not only on the history of the local community but also on community views of the broader world. The Hebrew Union Congregation in Greenville, Mississippi, keeps an exhibit titled "A Century of History" in the library of its temple. It looks at community politics and major events through the lens of the congregation, demonstrating the centrality of the Jewish community in Greenville. From Greenville's first mayor, a member of Hebrew Union, to the flood of 1927, all events are discussed from the perspective of the curator, also a member of Hebrew Union. "A Century of History," like many community exhibits, interprets the history of war through the experiences of the community's veterans, arranging sub-themes not by broad historical categories but by the collections of individual veterans. For example, the exhibit's striking section on World War II includes the story of one veteran who assisted in the liberation of Dachau in 1945.[19] Community curators allow for and even encourage individualized perspectives on local, national, and international history. The effect is distinct from academic exhibition, which employs ideas about objectivity that govern academic discourse.

The entrepreneurial exhibition has close ties to small business and perpetuates craft traditions. It may be located in the same building as a small business, but the gallery and the objects themselves are set apart from the business activity (unlike vernacular exhibitions, which occur in the same space as retail or service activities). The exhibit is usually funded by the small business, and, topically, these exhibits reflect the interests and collections of the business owners and are characterized by the features of small businesses: intimate spaces and face-to-face conversation with owners. Scholars have yet to significantly address the entrepreneurial exhibition.

Jim Anderson created the Olde Mill House Printing Museum in 1995. As a printer himself, he knows about the possibilities and limits of print communication. The digital age was his inspiration for creating the printing museum. He observed the changes in the trade he had been in since he was a teenager and took on the role of saving and explaining the old methods of printing. His collections include inked blocks, iron hand letterpresses, and platen letterpresses, all operational. His desire to bring his printing business from Tampa and create the museum in Old Homosassa was inspired in part

Figure 2.3. Printing press at the entrance of the Olde Mill House Printing Museum. (Old Homosassa, Florida. Photo by author.)

by the presence of the sugar mill ruins in this small Florida town. Descended from cane workers, Mr. Anderson identifies strongly with Florida's African American past.[20] He blended these interests in his museum and can move smoothly from talking about printing press technology to ethnic identity. He begins each tour with a word from an antique dictionary; he chooses this word based on his visitors' interests, which he discusses before the tour. Each tour stresses the human ability to communicate, which he sees as the ultimate message of the artifacts. Such attention to individual visitors is a trait characteristic of the small business, service-focused environment, and visitors respond positively. The dominant theme that emerges from interviews with visitors at the Printing Museum is, in the words of one patron, "Jim breathes life into these artifacts"[21]; the significance of the visit is to learn about history and make personal connections with a person who knows about it.

Entrepreneurial exhibits merge trade history with personal history. The Middlefield Cheese Factory Museum exhibits blend the history of cheesemaking with the history of the cheesemaker. The exhibits focus on the business and family history of the factory, and explain the process of

Figure 2.4. Display, including diplomas and the family Bible, on cheesemaker Hans Rothenbuhler at the Middlefield Cheese Factory Museum. (Middlefield, Ohio. Photo by author.)

cheese production, the founding of the Middlefield Cheese Factory, and the personal histories of Ann and Hans Rothenbuhler, the company's founders. The display includes antique cheesemaking equipment, art depicting cheesemakers, Hans Rothenbuhler's 1947 Swiss master cheesemaker's diploma, a factory model, a Rothenbuhler Bible, and a model of the Rothenbuhler home; some displays were professionally produced, while others were more decidedly homemade. The main theme is that the Rothenbuhlers combined Christian faith, hard work, and skill to create a successful business. The sign entrance to the museum/cheese shop evokes the importance of both cheese and religion: "It is written *Man Cannot Live By Bread Alone* Luke 4:4".[22]

Entrepreneurial exhibits sometimes grow from initial efforts in vernacular exhibition. Such is the case for the American Sanitary Plumbing Museum in Worcester, Massachusetts. Charles Manoog, owner of a plumbing supply company, retired from the business and began work on a museum to tell the history of plumbing in the United States. Using his business contacts with plumbers to build a collection, he created historical displays for the store. Later, Manoog's son created a stand-alone museum, which he now directs and curates with his wife, B.J. Manoog. Artifacts include a spigot dated to 1652, prison toilets, and historic dishwashers and showers. The exhibits also include historic tools of the trade. Trade schools use the museum to educate students on the history of plumbing and artisanal heritage.[23]

Entrepreneurial exhibitions demonstrate the importance of first-person accounts and face-to-face interactions in museums as well as the possibilities for designing small-space galleries and more intimate settings for larger museums.

Vernacular exhibitions are those that are integrated into non-museum settings like bars, restaurants, or barbershops.[24] Museal display and other activities mingle seamlessly. Users can discuss artifacts while eating, getting a haircut, or getting drunk. Using historic artifacts in a museum presentation, these exhibits represent the interests of owners or users. Visitors report liking vernacular exhibition because it makes them feel they are part of a tradition. Interviews conducted with patrons at Murphy's Bleachers—a museum bar next to Wrigley Field dedicated to Cubs history—show that visitors like the museum presentation because it operates on emotion, emphasizing their own participation in a continuing tradition. It helps legitimize their connection to a fan community.[25]

Scholarship on vernacular exhibitions is scarce indeed. Twenty years ago in their study of museum bars in the upper Midwest, Kurt Dewhurst and Marsha MacDowell identified the possibility of learning from museum bars:

> As a gathering place, the museum bar provides an opportunity for the objects assembled there to be invested with new meanings as well as convey a connect-

edness to past traditions. Usually developed through community participation, rather than the efforts of a single curatorial vision, the collection of objects and related folklore can provide a rich index of community life . . . .Understanding the cultural life of a museum bar therefore begins with fieldwork within the closed circle of museum bar patrons. Then can the objects be properly considered as part of the expressive local culture that deserves conservation.[26]

Other scholars have emphasized the community function of vernacular exhibition. In their discussion of "reliquary theming" in bars and restaurants, Alan Beardsworth and Alan Bryman emphasize that artifacts move the emphasis from consumption of food or drink to the experience of being in a meaningful space:

> With [reliquary theming], emphasis is placed upon the creation of an entertaining and appealing setting through the display of precious artifacts of known provenance. These artifacts are in fact 'relics' and their provenance links them directly to revered or heroic figures or to highly salient events or processes in the public domain. The presence of sacred relics introduces a sense of pilgrimage to the experience; the logic of the diner's attendance is as much to pay homage to the objects as to consume the food on offer.[27]

Documentation of vernacular exhibition appears in travel guides, authored with visitors in mind, not scholars. These guides document a stunning diversity of topic.[28]

Exhibits in non-museum settings make objects highly accessible. In fact, collections care is usually secondary to access. One restaurant museum provided a provocative case study of collections access. Billie and John Pappas, the owners of B&J's American Café in downtown LaPorte, Indiana, have re-created a restaurant from the middle decade of the last century, as their menu cover relates:

> As you sit in our restaurant today, the past surrounds you. We are pleased to have restored the restaurant back to its décor of the 1940s. Many of the items are original to the building including counters and stools, the buffet's tin ceiling, porcelain floors . . . .We have restored it as it was when the Pappas and Philon families owned it . . . from the 1920s to the early 1960s. The building has been in the Pappas family for over 8 decades.[29]

While the menu takes the visitor-patron through the architectural features of the restaurant, the primary impact of the rooms is in the photography on the walls and in the boxes on shelves in the banquet room. The restaurant is below a former photography studio, and the Pappases became the inheritors of not only photographic equipment (which they display in their restaurant) but also about fifty years of photo documentation of the LaPorte area's people and activities. The framed photographs on display are loosely

Figure 2.5. Photo collection in the banquet room at B&J's American Café. (LaPorte, Indiana, 2005. Photo by author.)

grouped according to type of photo (weddings, siblings, high school teachers, nature), and the banquet room is equipped with metal shelves holding boxes of photographs. The Pappases encourage visitors to peruse the photos. They have even provided people with copies of family photos that had been lost in fire or other disasters. In effect, the mid-century restaurant restoration functions as a highly accessible archive.

Some exhibitions evoke the past as a marketing tool to sell historic artifacts. This type of display has dual origins in merchandising and museums. Antique shops, secondhand stores, and flea markets offer this type of display. The image of the past presented usually does not go much more in depth than to connect to common perceptions (or misperceptions) of the past. The Liberty Antiques Mall in Lansing, Michigan, presents a good example. Among the many booths of antiques and collectibles for sale—booths stocked by different antiques dealers who took turns running the till and looking after the store—one shelf in a center aisle case contained about twenty nineteenth-century tintypes, each with its own post-it note. As expected, each note functioned as a price tag, referenced the dealer's code, and told what it was: "tintype." Unexpectedly, each post-it note also contained an interpretation of the subject matter and served as interpretive labels. Some were in a distinctive voice, reminiscent of nineteenth-century parlor culture, a gossipy, novel-of-manners type of voice:

"She's way too old for ringlets..."
"Almost a smile on this young aristocrat's face..."
"'Plain as the day is long'"[30]

The display demonstrates an interpretive sensibility, an effort to not just display a themed collection, but to assert its meaning in a historical context. While this particular effort is also one of marketing (it adds to the value by evoking the setting in which the objects were presumed to have circulated), it is also a teaching moment, a moment in which to engage its viewer in thought about the past. This antiques dealer teaches the antiques shopper that there were ill manners born of the culture of manners.

One noticeable trend in vernacular exhibition is parody: they make fun of the conventions of the exhibition medium. The Euclid Avenue Yacht Club, a bar in Atlanta, displays yachting and boating artifacts to play on the bar's reputation as a hangout for working-class bikers and not upper-class yachtsmen. The sheer impossibility of yachting in Atlanta parodies the traditional focus on place of historical exhibitions. Employees and patrons contribute to the collections regularly and assert proudly, "Our walls do talk."[31]

Vernacular exhibits are highly diverse, presenting scholars with opportunities to learn how visitors interact with historical exhibitions in multipurpose informal settings. This information would be relevant to larger museums' efforts to include the public in the exhibition development process.

Figure 2.6. "A city girl in all her finery." Tintypes display in the Liberty Antiques Mall. (Dewitt, Michigan, 2004. Photo by author.)

A revised typology of historical exhibition is necessary because, while scholars have approached the academic exhibit as normative, visitors have not. Academic exhibits may be reaching a point of professionalization that is starting to work against their own interest in making history relevant for contemporary visitors. Recent federal regulations that emphasize quantifiable educational outcomes, as well as much of the prescriptive literature, have emphasized exhibit development an act of marketing, a tool for producing the commodity "learning."[32] In getting large federal grants, exhibit developers must constantly, through rounds of formative, remedial, and summative evaluation, prove that visitors are "getting" their message. While much of this evaluation is highly useful, it has created a climate in which visitors may be lacking what they like best about history exhibits: intimacy with the past. Exhibits in small museums and in non-museum settings are intimate not only because the artifacts are highly accessible, but also because their connection to them is less mediated by institutional and academic authority. This does not mean that professional curators and museum educators are obsolete—far from it. It does mean, however, that professionals and nonprofessionals have a great deal to teach one another.

To fully understand the role of historical exhibition in the United States, we need to explore the medium in its diverse forms, particularly the ways in which visitors take meaning from them. This work is especially important for community, entrepreneurial, and vernacular exhibits, which have been neglected by scholars but not by visitors. Museum educators have been studying the ways in which visitors learn in large museums since the late nineteenth century. In the twentieth, increasing visitor demands, higher professional standards, and accountability pressures beginning with the Elementary and Secondary Education Act of 1965 combined to make the academic form of exhibition more distinct from others.[33] The growth of heritage tourism, paired with lively public discussion on the meaning of identity in America, has contributed to an increase in historical exhibitions in settings outside the large professionalized museums. Historical, sociological, and ethnographic methods have a great deal of potential for comparative work on learning in different museum settings. Visitors are aware of the real distinctions among exhibition types, but unlike scholars, they pay attention to the smaller, less professionalized exhibits. They report learning from—or being inspired by—all types. One couple, seasoned visitors who had been to the major museums of the United States and Europe, visited Da Yoopers Tourist Trap and Museum and reported it was a relief to think about history and culture without having to display the genteel appreciation they thought the "great museums" expected of them. Da Yoopers Museum let them get over their "museumed out" fatigue and helped to open their minds to new ways of looking at artifacts.[34]

Community, entrepreneurial, and vernacular exhibits make visitors comfortable, but they do not necessarily encourage complacency. In fact, they often encourage visitors to cross boundaries, to communicate with those outside their own social groups and understand history from another's perspective. They are public—in that anyone can see them—but they are also private, because their curatorial approaches are individualized. They make no claim to objectivity but instead offer history "from our point of view." These exhibit types are the ones that fully respond to Americans' interest in what Roy Rosenzweig and David Thelen termed "intimate" history.

3

Community Exhibition:
History, Identity, and Dialogue

Penderlea is a small rural community in southeastern North Carolina. Its roots can be traced to 1934, when it became the first farming homestead community established by the Subsistence Homesteads Division of the Department of the Interior. As part of the New Deal, the idea was to relocate families suffering from lack of employment to a central area and provide federal assistance to create infrastructure, housing, and truck farming and manufacturing opportunities. Local real estate developer Hugh McRae sold land to the government and acted as its first manager. Families had to apply to live there and meet the requirements; they had to be white, Protestant, married, and poor. They had to demonstrate their respectable moral character and pass a physical exam. The first "settlers" came in 1934, even before the houses were complete. They continued to come in over the next ten years, eventually filling around three hundred homes. Each home had indoor plumbing, electricity, and four to six rooms. The outbuildings included a barn, henhouse, pig barn, and smokehouse. Before the federal government pulled its support in 1944, it had created a school, a furniture factory, and a hosiery factory. Starting in 1944, the federal government began selling parts of Penderlea to private homeowners and companies. The residents dwindled in number as the factories closed or scaled back and small farming became less and less profitable. Today, about one hundred of the homes remain, including one that serves as the Penderlea Homestead Museum.[1]

While critics of the New Deal in the 1940s called Penderlea a failure because the community could not support itself—as its designers had intended—with the combination of truck farming and factory work, residents of Penderlea emphasize its ultimate success as a place where people got along and raised their children well. Resident Ann Cottle explained community life as she remembered it: "I would ride on the wagon to the mill with my Daddy to pick out the feed sacks I wanted for my clothes. And I was proud of my clothes . . . we all were . . . Penderlea was a wonderful place to grow up because we were all the same. We did not have money, but we were rich in love, food, and shelter. We children had everything we needed; we just didn't realize at the time how hard it was on our parents."[2] A visit to the Penderlea Homestead Museum gives that exact message. The house features a restored and re-created kitchen, bathroom, bedrooms, enclosed porch, and parlor. From the sewing patterns on the porch to the clothes in the closet, each object has a story, and chances are visitors will get a first-person account of having turned a pattern and a feed sack into a new dress.

Current and former residents rely heavily on community memory in the interpretation of all objects. They gather yearly for Homestead Day to tell and retell stories of growing up on Penderlea (the preposition is not "at" or "in" but "on" Penderlea). Guides know the people who wore the

Figure 3.1. Sewing patterns used by women on the Penderlea Homestead. (Penderlea Homestead Museum, Penderlea, North Carolina. Photo courtesy of North Carolina ECHO, State Library of North Carolina, Department of Cultural Resources.)

clothes, went to the dance described in the newspaper clipping, cooked on the stove, and played the piano. Depending on the guide, visitors will learn little about the discriminatory policies that led to a whites-only, Protestant-only living environment; nor will they learn about the criticism the federal government endured as the result of homesteads. They will, however, learn a great deal about day-to-day life on Penderlea, the main staple in historical memory of the town, interpretations that circulate on the wonders of getting a taste of what life was like out of poverty. Residents expressed joy over indoor plumbing and electricity, over plastered walls and modern kitchens. While the federal government went to great lengths to ascertain their poverty, residents felt rich with the new amenities. This feeling stayed in their memories and informed the creation of exhibits at the Penderlea Homestead Museum. Like countless other local history exhibits across the nation, the exhibits at Penderlea represent history from a place-based community's perspective. While local communities all over the nation intersected with the economies, policies, and social and cultural practices of other communities and even nations, the main purpose of community history exhibits is to emphasize community life from the residents' perspectives, not the changes over time in the broader social, political, or economic environment. The community exhibit is not a historical monograph; it is a memoir made tactile and visible.

The visitor experience at Penderlea Homestead Museum demonstrates some key features of the community exhibit. First, community exhibits are conceived and created by people who have lived the historical subject, who descend from those who lived it, or who identify strongly with the place that was shaped by the heritage being presented. Their curatorial choices are informed by experiential knowledge first, followed by more traditional historical methods. The curators are telling "their story." Second, the institutions themselves are flexible, depending on individual guides' memories and interests. Community exhibits take a decidedly informal approach to visitor learning, and at Penderlea Homestead Museum, the guide even sat at the kitchen table with visitors, as if they were guests in her home.

In many ways, the Penderlea Homestead Museum is representative of small museums in the United States: closely identified with place or community, run by volunteers with first-hand knowledge of the history, and visited regularly. When the federal government left its company town, the artifacts, the records, and many of the people remained. Like many sites of social history, the Penderlea Homestead Museum represents a collective memory of a time when industry was present, when jobs, however difficult, were more readily available. Historical display was a logical choice for this community. Many scholars would term this museum, and the many others like it in the American landscape, "local." Its funding comes from the community, the scope of its mission is to educate people about "this place." Its epistemology is a blend of indigenous and academic knowledge. The term "local," however, has connotations that are not necessarily helpful in understanding this type of exhibition. Being one of "the locals" implies ignorance, naïveté, lack of sophistication and worldview. "Locals" are either derided for their lack of cosmopolitanism or romanticized for their innocence. Either connotation implies disrespect and obfuscates the complicated functions of the past in American communities. The alternative term from anthropology is "indigenous curation," used by Nick Stanley in *Being Ourselves for You: The Global Display of Cultures* in 1998 and adapted from Sidney Moko Mead's 1983 "Indigenous Models of Museums in Oceania."[3] Christina Kreps uses the concept to refer to conservation practices that predate the Eurocentric museum model.[4] The term is also highly useful in understanding history museums created by those not considered "first peoples," those whose heritage dates more recently to the place being interpreted, but who have often been isolated from the dominant culture by geography, ethnicity, or class. "Indigenous," in this usage, refers to the construction of knowledge by community groups. "Curation," in this usage, refers to a community's agency; it is active in its construction of history. Unlike exhibits prepared by professional curators with more academic goals, community exhibits emerge from curators whose identities are profoundly informed by the history presented in the exhibition. They employ, in Stanley's term, "indigenous" curatorial techniques.

Evidentiary claims in community exhibits are varied and hybrid. Scholarship, memories, nostalgia, experience, community exigencies, and rumor work together to inform interpretation of artifacts for community exhibits. Some are highly dependent on academic knowledge; others are more suspicious of that knowledge and rely more heavily on experiential evidence or community oral tradition. This hybrid epistemology—uniquely applied according to economic, political, and social conditions—motivates every curatorial and institutional decision of the museum offering indigenous exhibits. Amy Levin notes that nostalgia in particular can drive local museum interpretation: ". . . nostalgia can privilege the past over the present, and it has a complicated relationship with narratives of success and the American Dream. Nostalgia fosters the ideals of the American dream and the self-made man, even as it gestures at a happier, halcyon time, an age of innocence before the fall into the knowledge of urbanism and industrialism."[5] Community exhibits are best understood not by their adherence to professional exhibition standards and guidelines, but by the community desire for sovereignty and/or self-determination and by visitor understanding of it. Community exhibits appeal to visitors in ways that are different from academic or corporate exhibits; visitors see them as more personal, less scripted, and therefore more intimate.

Visitors find this intimacy inviting. The community exhibition's conversational tone encourages visitors to identify, sympathize, or empathize with people telling the details of their lives or of their ancestors' lives. While not academic in the sense of offering a full critique of the subject matter and providing broader context, the indigenous exhibit is valuable in its ability to facilitate intergroup dialogue. While visitors would never pull off the highway, knock on a stranger's door, and ask to be told personal history, visitors will stop the car for a local museum. Community exhibits are the parlors of the locale.

HISTORY OF LOCAL HISTORY EXHIBITION

While local history exhibits in the nineteenth century appeared in settings as diverse as fairs, national museums, and freak shows,[6] the local history museum—with its emphasis on artifacts related to pioneers and founders—emerged in the mid-nineteenth century. The popularity of local artifact displays was related to both settlement and national identity. Writers of local history sought to promote settlement in their communities, while members of the professional class sought to define the "American" character against lower-class immigrant cultures. In 1876, even the president called for increased attention to local history.[7] Historian Patricia West explains middle-class women's efforts in this field as an outgrowth of their prescribed roles as keepers of the home, that during the 1860s and 70s, women created "history exhibits featuring domestic scenes in service of particular social agendas and aligning historic preservation with their conventional roles as reformers." Their efforts in delineating the centrality of white, middle-class women's roles in the formation of the nation continued to gain momentum, and by the 1890s new house museums organized at a rate of two a year.[8] The emergent field of ethnography led credence to exhibitions of locality, even if through the patrician self-image they transformed into pioneer stories, as the Sanitary Fairs and expositions in the latter half of the nineteenth century set the standard for "learned" displays of culture and history.[9]

As career historians in universities increasingly sought to distinguish themselves from amateurs in the first two decades of the twentieth century, museum display of local history came to be seen as the province of amateurs. While the American Historical Association (AHA) formed in 1884 with a collaboration of historians from without and within the university setting, differences began to emerge that eventually split professionals into two camps, differences historian David Russo terms "narrative treatment versus philosophical or analytical treatment."[10] Museum display fell away from the overview of the American Historical Association by 1940, when AHA members representing historical societies broke from the parent organization to form the American Association for State and Local History (AASLH), which dedicated itself to historical pursuits in museums, libraries, and historical societies outside of academe.[11] AHA members largely ignored museums between 1940 and the birth of the new social history in the 1960s; this period of AASLH's focus on serving the historical needs of nonprofessionals, according to historian Denise Meringolo, "marks the first moment when public historians failed to measure up to history's professional standards."[12] While academically trained public historians focused on history in the National Parks and "viewed all regional histories as potentially contributing toward a sense of national culture,"[13] amateurs continued creating local history exhibits, primarily for local audiences, especially schoolchildren.[14] In the 1960s, local museums began to receive attention from academics interested in community studies, urban studies, and social history. The American bicentennial, and the popularity of the *Roots* miniseries and the Foxfire books reignited interest in local history by the 1970s.[15] At the same time the growth of graduate programs in public history provided a crop of professionals to manage local resources. This process of professionalization of local history is ongoing, creating an eclectic style of American local exhibition. Far from their patrician roots, local history curators are a diverse lot. Some have advanced degrees, while others have little formal education at all. Exhibition styles, however, are just as responsive to community needs whether they are created by professionals or amateurs. What makes community exhibition different from local exhibition is not the educational background of the curator; rather, it is that the historical subject profoundly informs the identity of its curator.

SOVEREIGNTY AND COMMUNITY EXHIBITION

Like Roy Rosenzweig and David Thelen's subjects who focused not on the grand narratives of U.S. history but on the local, personal connections to the past, the creators of community exhibits are motivated to display by the need to "tell the story from our point of view," and are quite candid about not adhering to the historical profession's objectivity values.[16] The collective "our" is most often dictated by place, but it can also be ethnic or religious. Forty respondents to a 2006 needs assessment survey of small history museums and sites offer some clues about the institutional features of local museums.[17] Of the forty respondents, a full thirty-two made explicit mention of place in their mission statements, such as "to preserve the history of, and educate people about the history of, the towns of Gold Run, Dutch Flat, Alta, Towle and Baxter and the surrounding area, all in Placer

County, California." Other place identifiers were geological ("the Cherokee Outlet," "coastal Georgia," or "San Bernadino Mountains"), city, town, or region ("Wichita Falls" or "northeast Tennessee") or a place/people combination ("African Americans in the rural communities along the Mississippi River" or the "settlers of Penderlea . . . and local farm history in rural North Carolina.") A few offered missions that stated simply "local history." Of the remaining eight, two made no mention of mission and six cited population groupings ("Czech heritage"), individuals ("the life of Cordell Hull") or industries ("the trolley industry"). The reported staffing levels were just about evenly split among the following types of staffing: entirely volunteer, one paid full-time staff member with any number of part-time staff or volunteers, and two or three paid staff with any number of part-time staff or volunteers. When asked to record their top two sources of funding, 75 percent reported admission fees and donations, while government was one of the top two funding sources for only 35 percent of reporting museums. Other sources included museum-sponsored fundraisers (32.5 percent), endowments (20 percent), grants (15 percent), historical society dues (15 percent), and museum shop revenue (12.5 percent). The place/community missions, paired with the low staffing levels and heavy reliance on revenue from visitors and supporters, affects communication at the community exhibit. The heavy presence of volunteers as well as willingness of staff to engage visitors in face-to-face communication ensures a more intimate exchange than those that occur in larger history museums. This intimacy, museum workers assert, is important to community identity or even sovereignty.

The motivation for people who create community exhibitions is not to contribute to a scholarly dialogue on the topic, the goal of academic exhibitions, articles, and monographs. Instead, community curators believe that exhibits help the community by representing their interests to outsiders, connecting elders to young people, building a sense of shared past, and bringing in tourist dollars. As Kammen so accurately states, "local historians are dependent on the community for information and new materials. An 'unreliable' local historian, one who embarrasses residents or makes them uncomfortable, will soon find documents unavailable and people unwilling to cooperate. . . . To ignore local expectations can be a self-defeating scenario, for we must continue to live among those about whom, or for whom, we write."[18] This reality, however, does not mean that indigenous curators unthinkingly follow community demands. First and foremost, communities are conflicted about their past; there is rarely a historical interpretation with which all agree. Second, community curators are not, as a general observation, meek or squeamish. They are active in promoting their own interpretations. Sometimes this means telling salacious stories of serial killers, while other times it means arranging genteel home tours with the "Gracious Homes Committee."[19] News coverage of historical society activity in the United States turns up more than one strong personality. The late Gordon Hodgin of Delta, Colorado, was known as "Mr. Delta" for his community activities: "he was a local storyteller, amateur historian, fundraiser and unstoppable civic promoter." Delta County Historical Society Museum Director Jim Wetzel recalled that Hodgin "sometimes didn't have all the facts right. He might embellish a little, but we never minded." Nevertheless, he "made history come alive for me," a friend reported, "He had a flair for storytelling."[20] Elain Egdorf, one of the founding members of the Homewood Historical Society, noted "I disliked history in school. It was memorizing. I figured if I needed a date or fact, I'd look it up." Her early dislike of history notwithstanding, she dedicated a significant portion of her adult life to community history and preservation, serving on local and state historical boards and leading a legal battle to save the house that became the society's museum in 1987. In 1999 she received a service award from the Illinois Humanities Council. Her transformation from unwilling student to history promoter came about with an epiphany on the meaning of history: "As I got into local history, I realized that history is you and me; history is all of us, is what's happening today....Fifty, [a hundred] years from now, people will be studying who we are. Everyone is important in some way to the fabric of their town. [We need to] wake up people to the diversity we have here, in ethnicity, economics, housing, architecture."[21] Marilyn Elliot, curator of the Columbus Historical Society Museum in New Mexico, entered civic work through activities at her children's school. She started at the museum as a volunteer and became curator in 1994. Her motivation is her commitment to communication across ethnic boundaries, modeled by her grandmother, who led the effort to integrate public schools in East Los Angeles.[22]

Community exhibition is often motivated by people who have been historically "othered," people whose histories have been told by those outside the community. For them, historical exhibition is one way to claim local control over heritage resources and to assert sovereignty. Such is the case with the exhibits at the Shoshone-Bannock Tribal Museum. Founded in 1985 as part of an initiative to diversify business activity at the Fort Hall Reservation, the museum is located near the I-15 exit by a restaurant, a gas station, a casino, a grocery store, and a gift shop, businesses dependent on both local and tourist dollars.[23] Like many small historical museums, the Shoshone-Bannock Tribal Museum struggled financially and closed for a short time. In 1993 it was reopened by volunteers, and by 1996, it had a paid manager. Significantly, the current manager attributes the museum's survival to the community's commitment to maintaining control of their history, for they "see a real need to tell our story from our point of view."[24]

This point of view is distinct from the stereotypes of American Indians held by a number of visitors and indeed by American culture at large.

Figure 3.2. Museum assistant April Eschief talks with a visitor about different types of powwow music. Face-to-face conversation is an important educational strategy at the Shoshone-Bannock Tribal Museum. (Fort Hall, Idaho, 2006. Photo by author.)

Volunteers and staff at the Shoshone-Bannock Tribal Museum report that visitors commonly ask to see the tipis in which the Shoshone-Bannock assumedly live. Museum manager Rosemary Devinney responds to this according to "who we are as a tribe": people who appreciate difference and who approach life with highly developed senses of humor. She explains how Shoshones and Bannocks adapted many areas of their lives to changing conditions, just like visitors do. She is an astute observer of people, and is skilled in responding to individual visitor questions according to the knowledge needs she perceives in each visitor. During an exit interview, one visitor finished the survey with tears provoked by the exhibition. Ms. Devinney noted visitors regularly respond to the exhibition this way. She uses her appreciation of difference to inform this and other interactions with visitors:

> I'm not sure what it is that sets them off emotionally. I've never asked. I have just simply tried to help people through it . . . . Because you know, that's just the way maybe some people react. I know my grandmother always said that "as

humans we have a certain nature about us." Some people are very emotional, you know, and that's just their nature. And you need to understand that.[25]

Ms. Devinney's approach to visitors is highly personal. She wants visitors to be comfortable enough to ask the questions they're really curious about. It is only in being asked if they live in tipis that she feels she can debunk that particular myth. Ms. Devinney is not the only one at the museum invested in the idea that face-to-face conversation with visitors can help the tribe. Delbert Farmer, former Tribal Chair, current Revenue Director for the tribe, and long-time museum supporter and volunteer, sees the museum's independence as akin to tribal sovereignty; its existence attests to the tribes' ability to self-determine. Explaining sovereignty is one of the keys to maintaining it. He addresses visitor groups about governmental and tribal issues, drawing on his experience in government. Rusty Houtz, museum volunteer, exhibition designer and artist, speaks to visitor groups about what the reservation was like in the 1930s and about his experience as a Hollywood stuntman and rodeo star. These approaches are very different in content, but the delivery is the same: education based on face-to-face conversational exchange with people who are living the results of the history being presented.[26]

The interpretation at the Shoshone-Bannock Tribal Museum responds to more than contemporary visitors' preconceived notions about American Indians. Devinney notes that scholars have had a role in hindering tribal self-determination:

> A lot of books have been written about us and I've read a lot of them; it seems to me that the people who are writing the books are looking through a window. And they are looking at tribes and they're thinking "Well, what are these people doing?" And they make their observations based upon their own values and they don't really understand what the native people's values are. So I think that's our goal here in the museum is to let them know, this is why we did this. This is what we were doing. And hopefully that will give us a better understanding of one another.[27]

Devinney's comments reflect the hybrid epistemology of the exhibitions themselves. Academic scholarship informs the interpretation, but it is filtered through and tested against personal experience and the oral tradition.

The physical structure and exhibit design are consistent with the goal of tribal control of history. The museum consists of an octagonal exhibit area connected to a gift shop/lobby in the center, with office space off from central public space. Visitors come in the front door, pay admission, sign the guest book, and move through the gallery in a circular path. Exhibits are on diverse topics including use of natural resources, the Oregon Trail, art, boarding school, language, the Lewis and Clark expedition, and the tribes' history of cattle ranching. Thematic emphasis is on adaptation, both economic and cultural. Exhibits range from scientific (the Oregon Trail exhibit is based on archaeological information and the fisheries exhibition uses biological language) to personal (an exhibit on the mother of one of the volunteers). Objects—taxidermy, beadwork, artifacts left by nineteenth-century Oregon Trail travelers—are either the property of the museum or are on loan from community members. Each case has a different design, which adds to the feeling of eclecticism in the gallery. Manager Rosemary Devinney points out that the eclecticism represents the tribe well, for it was part of their history to use available materials and adapt to various conditions.[28]

Volunteers who curate individual cases leave their own touches. While the labels are written in the third person, it is obvious individual volunteers put personal touches on the displays. The Daisy Ballard St. Clair Collection display includes family photos and items made from animals, each with a label in Shoshone: "Dentso 'Wo, Handgame Bones" or "WE'KWE'NAI'I, Bone Hide Scraper." The display on Effie Diggie Houtz, the mother of exhibit designer Rusty Houtz, includes family photos and items Mrs. Houtz made for the gift shop she ran in the mid-twentieth century. Museum

Figure 3.3. Exhibit cases at the Shoshone-Bannock Tribal Museum. Museum manager Rosemary Devinney explains that the eclecticism of design represents the community's tradition of using all available resources. (Fort Hall, Idaho, 2006. Photo by author.)

Manager Rosemary Devinney reports that this type of curation is consistent with Shoshone views of the material world:

> In our belief system, and our culture, most of the best things are buried with the people. It's our belief that one day when we go to meet the creator that we will be dressed in the finest and those are the things that we accumulate and collect through our lifetime. And after that, if the person has property they want to give, they'll usually give to grandchildren. So it's passed down. A lot of things are very, very special to people and they don't want to part with them.[29]

The lack of personal belongings led the museum to focus their exhibits on resource use, particular phases of change, and major events in tribal history, like the exhibits on schooling, cattle ranching, veterans, and the most recent "The Shoshone Meet Lewis and Clark."

Exhibit development reflects the institution's focus on self-determination. When a new project idea emerges, Devinney organizes the tribe's talents. Delbert Farmer, well traveled and an avid museum goer, provides thematic consultation as well as financial direction. Devinney and volunteers conduct research and develop the idea, while artist Rusty Houtz does design work. Artists and craftspeople from the community provide fabrication and installation services. This development process invests community members in the museum, and, as Devinney puts it, demonstrates "that our people are so talented."[30]

While the Shoshone have traditions relating to material items that differ from traditional Euro-American ones, they also have something in common with other curators of community exhibits: they do not want the belongings of their ancestors commodified by others. The Munising Woodenware exhibit at the Alger County (Michigan) Historical Society Heritage Center demonstrates this same dynamic. This facility features a changing exhibit gallery, a fur trader's cabin re-creation, a gift shop offering artwork from local artists, an archive, and a meeting room with exhibits on the area's historic and contemporary industries. The Munising Woodenware exhibit is among these.

Munising Woodenware was a company operating in Munising from 1912 to 1955, creating a wide variety of hand-crafted wooden products from bowls and platters to tent stakes. Recently, Munising Woodenware became "collectible," making the exhibit difficult to create. While the other exhibits of local industry employ the prescribed professional authoritative voice, the Woodenware section breaks through the guise of objectivity to make direct appeals to the visitor, such as this label: "Unfortunately, there are many examples of Munising Woodenware which are not part of this exhibit. If you own a piece we don't have, we hope that you'll consider donating or bequeathing it to the museum for public display and preservation."

Figure 3.4.   Products in the Munising Woodenware exhibit at the Alger County Histori-cal Society. (Munising, Michigan, 2004. Photo by the author.)

Other interpretation also features the act of collection: "Munising Wood-enware has become a popular collectible around North America. It is not unusual to find it on 'E-Bay.' Especially prized are pieces in their original packaging or those with "Munising" brand burned into them." What fol-lows, and is given equal typographical weight on the label, is a list of people who contributed their pieces to the collection rather than selling them on a lucrative national market. Interpretation of World War II tent stakes also gives equal typographical weight to the fact that the donor bought them on eBay and donated them.[31] Interpretation that gives such prominence to the act of acquisition conceives of the visitor as a possible partner in the com-petition between the people who (in some cases literally) *made* this history and those who seek to use it as a market investment. It is tension between social classes as well as a battle between the rural, local creation of history and the national economy's appropriation of it. The exhibition practice of giving equal weight to the local control of history makes the exhibit an act of community assertion as much as an act of public education.

Sometimes local history museums with community exhibits emerge out of a lack of multiple perspectives in local history resources. Community museums of African American history sometimes fall into this category. Despite being a museum only large enough to accommodate twenty-five

visitors at a time, the River Road African American Museum in Donaldsville, Louisiana, attracts visitors from all over the United States because it
offers "information about slavery and freedom from a local perspective."[32]
Visitors appreciate such efforts significantly, as one visitor wrote admiringly
of the River Road Museum's founder Kathe Hambrick, under the subhead-
ing "Passionate Historian":

> Another shining local star is Kathe Hambrick. Hambrick founded the **River
> Road African American Museum**, which is also located on Donaldsonville's
> main street. A former corporate gal, she left the suit world behind to start
> a museum that would showcase the contributions of African Americans in
> Louisiana's Mississippi River Valley. She dedicates much of her time to work-
> ing with school children, teaching them about the hardships of slavery and the
> realities of the Underground Railroad. It's evident the museum and its mission
> are Hambrick's passion.[33]

Such unique offerings have emerged in areas in which the supply of opportunities for learning African American history in an informal setting has
not kept up with the demand.[34]

Church anniversaries and memorabilia displays demonstrate a con-
gregation-focused approach that emphasizes continuity in community
values. Christian churches celebrating anniversaries will have memorabilia
displays along with "old-time" days in which congregants dress in period
clothing. When First Baptist in Fairmont, North Carolina, celebrated its
200th birthday in 1992, its members came to church dressed circa 1792,
which meant men spent weeks cultivating the right beards and moustaches.
The celebration included horse-drawn carriage rides, artifacts, a dinner, and
"historical 'show-and-tell' gatherings." The event took on features of the
family reunion, with a diagram of members and their lineages described by
the church's pastor: "'You've heard of a family tree. Well, this is a church
family tree.'"[35] Congregations rarely wait for two hundred years, however.
The Holy United Methodist Church in Houston, Texas, created a memorabilia display for its fiftieth anniversary in 2004.[36] The Second Church of
Newton, Massachusetts, used an anniversary display of church-related artifacts to launch an art gallery in 1981. The Chapel Gallery hosts one show
per month organized by a church committee.[37]

Rather than using temporary displays, the Hebrew Union Congregation
in Greenville, Mississippi, maintains a permanent exhibition in the library
of the temple. Like the Shoshone-Bannock Tribal Museum displays, it
mingles national and international events with community and personal
history and is less nostalgic than the "old-time" celebrations held by Christian churches. Covering over a century, the display teaches about the Jewish
community of Greenville in the late nineteenth century and its significant
contributions to the town's growth, including its first mayor, a member of

Hebrew Union Congregation. The displays, intermingled with reference works in the library, compellingly cover World War II and the Holocaust. Several of these are organized by collectors, who provide artifacts and first-hand accounts of their experiences in World War II. Of particular interest in this exhibit are cases displaying the belongings—weapons, medals, newspaper clippings of Melvin Lipnick, who participated in the liberation of Dauchau in 1945.[38] Congregation Beth Ahabah in Richmond, Virginia, offers highly professionalized displays related to its two-hundred-year history. Located next to its sanctuary but operating as a stand-alone museum, the Beth Ahabah Museum and Archives offers exhibits that blend personal, community, national, and international history.[39]

Sometimes local history museums assert community identity based on folklore. Such is the case with the Hell's Belle exhibit at the LaPorte Historical Society Museum in LaPorte, Indiana. Belle Gunness was a Norwegian immigrant who lived in the rural area outside LaPorte from 1902 until her disappearance in 1908. She lured men to her house (some through ads in Norwegian newspapers), stole their belongings, murdered them, and buried them in the hog pen behind her house. When a farm hand burned down the house in 1908, investigators found the remains of eighteen people, including Ms. Gunness's children, on the farm. Subsequent legend raised the number to forty.[40] The Belle Gunness farm became the stuff of local legend, a tourist attraction, and a place teens dared each other to enter late at night. The wheelbarrow, in which Ms. Gunness presumably carried bodies to the hog yard, is on display, as well as one exterior wall of her cabin, where those who dared carved their initials in the years between Belle's disappearance and the museum's accession of the wall. Personal belongings from the murdered men were recovered from her house and are on display. The interpretation covers the investigation and subsequent growth of the legend of "Hell's Belle," "The Gunness Monster," "Bluebeard in Skirts!" and "The Case of the Butchering Widow." One label mentions that postcards featuring Belle Gunness are on sale at the gift shop, and asks visitors to "Buy one—if you dare!"[41] The Gunness story and its attendant folklore is an important feature of the small museum located in the courthouse building, and the museum is planning events to mark the anniversary of Belle's disappearance, "with dignity and taste, hopefully," in the words of the museum's assistant curator. Grave markers for the victims and well as forensic inquiry into the identity of the body in Belle Gunness's grave are on the commemoration agenda.[42]

The prominence of this story in the town's history speaks not just to the gruesome events on the Gunness farm between 1902 and 1908 but the changes in local historians' foci. Such exhibits directly confront the notion that local history exhibits will necessarily tell the stories that put the community in the best possible light. The growth of ghost tours is evidence that

Figure 3.5. Human model depiction of serial killer Belle Gunness through a window in the wall of her house. Note the initials carved onto the house by generations of "those who dared" get close to it. (LaPorte County Historical Society, LaPorte Indiana, 2005. Photo by author.)

some local historians have departed significantly from genteel boosterism. Historical society members at museums commonly repeat the tragic and horrendous events of the community, especially if it has the makings of a ghost story. Drug addiction, child abuse, murder, and even amateur midnight exhumations are subjects local historians highlight. One Illinois historical society has rich material: "So many frightening incidents have taken place in McHenry County that the historical society re-enacts them—a hodgepodge of homicides, suicides, and other tragic deaths. The McHenry County Historical Society Museum is dark as a ghoul leads visitors through vignettes that illuminate an aspect of the area's past."[43] Unlike the plantation museums that romanticize or minimize slavery,[44] ghost walker tours give gruesome details of the horrors and tortures of slaves.[45] This trend indicates a decidedly different direction in local history away from civic promotion, although it does not always have the educational goal of making visitors question the systems that allowed and encouraged humans to mistreat each other. The lesson is generalized on the human condition, such as that provided by McHenry County Historical Society administrator Nancy Fike: disturbing occurrences of the past "tell us that there has always been human misery and there has always been a seamy side and a tragic side of life."[46] Often it is about appealing to visitors' senses in an age when the gruesome is a significant feature of movies and primetime television.[47]

Not only are curators of community exhibits willing to get personal in matters of death, addiction, and abuse, they are also rather candid on their views of religion. In their national survey of American conceptions of the past, Rosenzweig and Thelen found religion to be a significant force in shaping many Americans' relationship to history. The authors could identify about 5 percent of their national sample as evangelical Christians "for whom a Christian identity both shaped and was shaped by a particular understanding of the past."[48] Community exhibits reflect fewer concerns about reaching the religiously diverse audiences of larger museums, and some even use the exhibition as evangelical medium. The Billy Sunday Visitors Center uses a curatorial voice that conceives of its audience as fellow Christians, or even as fellow evangelical Christians. Located in Sunday's former tabernacle near the Billy Sunday Home in Winona Lake, Indiana, the Visitors Center houses exhibits displaying the markers of professionalism: a short documentary introduction, conservation-minded mounts, a full re-creation, interactive elements, a radial-random floor plan, and immersion experiences. Like most professional exhibits, the introduction area delivers the main theme: in this case, that Billy Sunday overcame a life of sin to devote his life to preaching, eventually reaching a hundred million people. The emphasis on numbers indicates curatorial assumption of the audience's familiarity with a major goal of evangelism, saving the masses from sin. The main theme text from the label *Billy Sunday: America's*

Baseball Evangelist notes he spoke to one hundred million and "saw over one million come to faith in Christ." The central object in the introduction, a Plexiglas box full of salt, reinforced the importance of numbers. The label explains:

How Many is One Hundred Million?
This cube contains approximately one hundred million grains of salt. If each grain was a living, breathing person, one could see the number of people to whom Billy Sunday preached over the course of this life. No human being, before or since Billy Sunday, has spoken to as many people without the use of television, radio, or public address loudspeakers. He typically spoke to groups of about five to ten thousand, two or three times per day, six days per week during his campaigns.[49]

Such an approach is consistent with the professional practice of building on visitors' existing knowledge. Relying on visitors' adherence to the goals of evangelism, the curatorial voice makes consistent connections to the positive value of Sunday's work. The only section that recognizes diverse viewpoints is the display of objects found in the Sunday home that provide evidence the Sundays may have partaken of drink, dance, and agnostic literature. The label interpreting a 78 record of dance music, cordial glasses, a brandy snifter, and an agnostic text with Sunday's notes reads: "All of the items in this case were found in the Sunday's [sic] possessions in Mount Hood. While none of these artifacts offers conclusive evidence to support Billy's critics, the presence of these objects in the Sunday home does raise new questions."[50] Even as it conforms to the more academic practice of acknowledging opposing views, it also departs, however, by privileging an interpretation that serves evangelical goals.

Personal histories mingle with other types of history in collections displayed to the public from collectors' homes. These represent the ultimate in public/private confusion through historical display. Bruce Davis of Framingham, Massachusetts, opens his home, an 1890s Colonial painted pink, to visitors on the local historical society tour. No scion of genteel decorating, Davis instead highlights his collections. He has rooms full of Mickey Mouse items, cowboy artifacts, dolls, sleds, and even an Egyptian room, complete with a pharaoh mural he painted himself. His collections policy? "I'm addicted to pretty things . . . It has to have an expression, character. It has to be interesting or I don't want it."[51] Mickey McGowan's rented home was known in 1989 as The Unknown Museum, a collection of twentieth-century popular culture artifacts including dolls, televisions, "a group of toy atomic reactors from the 1940s that proclaim 'You can measure fallout radiation and survive!',", games, lunch boxes, and bathroom scales.[52] Journalist Paul Liberatore recently found McGowan living in San Rafael, California, having moved "the fifty truckloads of vintage stuff he hauled away when

Figure 3.6.   Central object at stop wall: salt grains representing the number of people to whom Sunday preached. (Billy Sunday Visitors Center, Winona Lake, Indiana. Photo by author.)

he left Mill Valley" in 1989 when his rented house was demolished for a new condominium project. Liberatore called the Unknown Museum a relic from when Mill Valley was "undiscovered and inexpensive, when a bunch of eccentric artists could rent a storefront downtown for $200 a month and leave the place unlocked day and night and nobody took a thing." McGowan took the gentrification as a sign to scale back the public side of his collection. While still collecting, he rarely gives tours.[53] His collections policy continues to be guided by nostalgia: "It's all the things that people have lived with . . . it's really about what these things meant to us. Nostalgia is nothing to be afraid of. There's a comfort in the past."[54]

As can be seen in these examples, community curators are not always worried about the objectivity issue. They are quite honest about exhibiting history as "our story" or even "my story." Whether collective identity is defined by religion, place, ethnicity, or even individual eccentricity, community curators openly express the ways in which that identity informs the interpretation. It is this articulation of identity that visitors find compelling.

COMMUNITY EXHIBIT VISITORS

The epistemological hybridity that characterizes the community exhibition is appealing to visitors. They understand the exhibition in comparison to other, larger exhibits and mass media, seeing the indigenous exhibit as more "authentic" or "real" because it emerges from the people whose identity is profoundly informed by this history. This does two things. First, it demonstrates that visitors may be oversaturated with highly polished cultural products.[55] Second, it places historical exhibition within the same frame of understanding as other cultural tourism, the phenomenon in which "the locals" display an identity while simultaneously living it, something Nick Stanley terms "being ourselves for you."[56] Identity is more than a topic of conversation between visitors and curators, though; curatorial identity is one of the reasons visitors engage the exhibits. These identities could be placed within the context of subverting the traditional relationships between museums and ethnographic subjects. Indeed, scholars of museums have produced a great deal of work on performance and the ethnographic artifact.[57] These studies, however, typically focus on ethnographic objects managed by large, dominant culture institutions. Scholarly overemphasis on the tourist gaze and the ethnographic performance of the visited, however, downplays the complicated dynamics of curator-visitor communication. In the private history exhibit, the exchanges between curator and visitor about identity complicate the traditional ethnographic dichotomy between those doing the gazing and those being gazed upon as well as the unequal power relationships traditionally informing the curator/

visitor relationship. The very fluidity of these categories in the private history exhibit contributes to a visitor experience that is significantly less formal than a visit to a larger museum.

The Shoshone-Bannock Tribal Museum exhibits provide a useful case study for analyzing these issues of visitor/curator relationships. Interviews with visitors and curators demonstrate that, in the space of the small museum, curators and visitors engage in conversations that challenge traditional curator/visitor and self/other hierarchies.[58] The small museum is a public space in that any one can come in and use it, but it has a more private, informal character than most large museum exhibits, however, and visitors are more likely to start conversations with curators.

Visitors were not making the Shoshone-Bannock Tribal Museum their main objective for the day. Three-quarters saw the sign on the highway and decided to stop, validating the museum's decision to advocate for more directional signage on the state highway.[59] Other visitors had read about the museum from a guidebook, brochure, or map, while others had heard about it by word of mouth. Visitors reported multiple reasons for deciding to visit, most of which were general curiosity or an established interest in American Indian history or history in general. Of the whole sample, only one was a repeat visitor.

Visitors spent about forty minutes on average in the exhibit room. Most spent an additional five to fifteen minutes talking with staff or looking at books in the lobby. When asked the main theme of the exhibits, more than half (N=14) said that the main theme had to do with features of tribal history, but visitors cited different features. Typical responses included: "To honor the life and the way and the art of the people," "To show the various ways people made a living," "There is a lot of local pride here," "There was a great culture," "How hardy they were," and "To inform you of Indian culture, history, and artifacts." Six visitors cited the Lewis and Clark expedition as the main message or one of the main messages, probably due to the dominance of the special exhibit on that topic. Four visitors cited cultural difference as the main theme, which reflects that these visitors picked up on the dominant themes cited above and blended them into one cohesive theme. One visitor noted "Indians were a wonderful people who lived with the earth and got short ended by the white man. White men try to change everybody and that's not right. People should be loved for themselves." Another responded with "The differences between the two cultures and the little effort that was made to connect. All the effort was made by the Indians."[60] Visitors reported being motivated to learn history. When asked to rate their interest in learning history on a 1–10 scale, they reported an average interest of 8.88. They reported being interested in a' diversity of objects, with the highest number (N=9) citing beadwork as the most interesting photo or object, while others cited animal displays, Lewis and Clark, and photos of ranches or schools.

In most ways, they were museum visitors engaging typically with exhibits, but visitors' interactions with the exhibits themselves were only part of the process, and perhaps the less important part. The museum is set up so that visitors do not enter or leave the exhibit space without passing a volunteer or curator. Staff members at the Shoshone-Bannock Tribal Museum are proactive in encouraging conversation. When visitors emerge from the gallery, staff members ask "What do you think?" or "What are your questions?" The intimate space of the gallery/lobby/gift shop is a place in which people feel comfortable talking. It took little prompting for conversations to begin. This could result in something as brief as a two-minute discussion of colors in the beadwork or as extended as a forty-minute, reference-work-assisted discussion of the relationship between a nineteenth-century Danish photographer and her Shoshone-Bannock subjects. The presence of gift shop items like books, artwork, or CDs prompted some discussion, like one conversation about different types of powwow music. Others were more personal and philosophical, with staff and visitors discussing different Americans' perceptions of heritage and its relationship to personal responsibility.[61] The willingness of museum staff members to present themselves as individuals and not as unquestionable institutional authorities provoked visitor engagement. The exhibit content, which is honest and epistemologically hybrid, the close and intimate space of the lobby area, and the proactive approach to communication taken by staff resulted in a high level of visitor engagement.

A 2006 survey of small museums confirmed the reasons visitors like learning history in these settings. When asked "What do visitors like best about your museum?" most responded citing specific artifacts, collections, or exhibits. Some cited specific experiences, like being able to climb to the top of a lighthouse, ride a streetcar, or pan for gold. One mansion museum staff member noted that visitors get insight into affluent lifestyles (lifestyles they do not have): "Our museum is located in an affluent neighborhood. I believe visitors think that our museum is a glimpse into what the adjacent houses might be like inside."[62] Insider knowledge was important to visitors in other cases as well. One museum reported visitors enjoyed "artifacts . . . relating to our heritage."[63] The Great Plains Welsh Heritage Museum reported that "one of our best programs is a re-enactment of early settlers telling their first person stories (by actual descendents standing by their ancestors' gravestones in the Welsh cemetery)." Many cited services that appealed to more basic human needs: connection to other people. "Friendly staff members and volunteers," "staff friendliness and knowledge," and the "small size, friendly volunteers and staff" are what appeal to visitors in these settings.

The IXL Museum in Hermansville, Michigan, is a case study in the personal interaction so common to the community exhibit. Hermansville,

Figure 3.7.   Familial intimacy in the museum setting. This label reads "NI-DDY NODDY. A reel to wind and measure yarn. This was made by Mrs. Joseph Birgy's Grandfather." (Fife Lake Area Historical Society, Fife Lake, Michigan, 2005. Photo by author.)

a town near Michigan's Wisconsin border, had a population of 1,041 in 2000. It has two museums: the Vietnam Veteran's Museum and the IXL Historical Museum. They are only open in the summer, when tourists begin to roam the area looking for camping, hiking, and fishing opportunities. Two weeks before the opening in 2006, I visited the IXL museum to find it still closed, but a volunteer opened the building, stated there was as yet no heat, but that we were welcome to give ourselves a tour. She handed us a tour book and pointed toward the first stop, the front entry room. We learned that the imposing building was an office of the Wisconsin Land and Lumber Company of Fond du Lac, Wisconsin, built in 1882–1883 to provide lumber to C. J. L. Meyer's sash and door company. We learned that "IXL" was the name of this branch company and was Meyer's way of asserting just that: "I excel." We went from room to room, learning how clerks distributed checks to lumbermen, how the secretary used a dictaphone, and that employees wore metal tags to identify themselves. We learned about billing and accounting in the Work Room. We looked at the switchboard and read how the company hired an operator who handled not only company calls but calls for other area businesses. Mimeoscopes and copypresses provided additional insight on late nineteenth-century office work. We went to the basement to learn about the family who lived there and provided all janitorial services for the building. We toured the upstairs, living quarters for clerks. The abundance of woodwork attested to the dominance of the lumber industry, as did the mill artifacts displayed in two rooms. In the company vault, we marveled at the abundance of company records: account books, maps, and journals.[64]

This "self-guided" tour turned out to be rather "other guided" as well, for in each area, volunteers and museum staff were working to prepare for the tourist season. At each stop, they ceased working to talk with us, sharing their insights not only into the history of IXL but also their own history of working there and discovering interesting features of the house and its history. They also shared their opinions on the process of curation. These conversations went even further when we met one volunteer who had grown up in this company town, her father an employee of IXL. She let us into the lone example of worker housing, a small house set up as it would have looked in the 1920s, and told us that it was difficult for her parents to be dependent on the company store, a childhood memory that still appeared vivid. The interactions throughout the building with people who descended from the earlier workers made this exhibit all the more present. The face-to-face conversations implied that the events depicted here shaped the lives of friends, not strangers, creating intimacy with visitors.

Behavioral observation and visitor surveys at the Shoshone-Bannock Tribal Museum as well as visitor identification of interaction with staff as a high point of their visit to small museums affirm the unique role community exhibits play in American life. While they are in public institutions, they encourage rather private conversations among strangers. Curators make personal connections to visitors, letting them into their experiences. Visitors, in turn, feel a shared sense of the past or gain sympathy for another's perspective. While objectivity may not be a dominant characteristic of community exhibits, dialogue is.

This dialogue is supported by its relationship to tourism. The highway sign that brought us to Hermansville and the IXL Museum—"Fine Food and History Museum"—indicates a significant role for the small museum. It is one way small communities can support their businesses. Even as the community exhibit works toward community self-definition by controlling its own heritage resources, the small museum cannot escape its dependence on funds brought from without the community. Intergroup dialogue functions to create better understanding among diverse groups of people. It is also salable. The exhibits that draw more heavily on salability are the subjects of the following two chapters.

4

Entrepreneurial Exhibition: Historical Display and the Small Business Tradition

The First Due Fire Museum, located in a shopping mall in suburban Hazelwood, Missouri, offers firefighting history from the firefighter's perspective. The museum's vision has a dual emphasis "to provide valuable public fire safety education and fire service history and memorabilia." The museum, funded by donors, primarily firefighters, firefighters' unions, and businesses related to firefighting, emphasizes interactivity and face-to-face conversation over label-driven interpretation. The objects and conversations are many; the labels are few. A highly accessible museum, the First Due holds hours typical of a mall but highly atypical of a museum run entirely by volunteers (in 2006, seventy-eight retired and current firefighters divvied up shifts at the museum). Museum founder and Hazelwood Fire Department Assistant Chief Erick Kiehl understands that attracting visitors is more likely if the museum is near other regularly used services. Explaining the museum's unique shopping mall location, Kiehl noted that "stand-alone fire museums usually only attract firefighters, never everyday people. It's easy for people to visit us here. They're out shopping, and they can come and learn something about firefighters and fire safety." It is accessible for children and offers many opportunities for tactile learning; according to Kiehl, "they can try on a coat and feel the weight of a nozzle."[1] Unapologetically celebratory of the profession, the exhibits teach, in the words of one visitor, "what firefighters throughout the years have had to endure while saving our unappreciative asses."[2] The museum's focus on service is clear. It raises money for charities and provides fire safety lessons for local schools. Even its website reminds one to check the battery in the smoke detector.[3]

The First Due Fire Museum offers entrepreneurial exhibits. They are "entrepreneurial" not because their purpose is to make money—although sometimes that may be part of it—but because they reflect the traditional role of small business as well as the role of the small business *person* as one who is committed to and reflective of community. Like many small businesses in the United States, the First Due Fire Museum has a strong commitment to the local community. Like small businesses, it depends largely on face-to-face communication between its users and its staff to cement ties and participate in transaction, whether social or monetary. To further the analogy, the spatial characteristics of exhibit both in its location (among commercial venues) and within the gallery itself (its different units arranged to maximize visitor choice) reflect those of small retail businesses in particular. One of the continuities of the history of small business in America is that while the small business itself has been criticized as inefficient, the small business *person* reflects the way in which Americans prefer to view themselves: independent, morally upstanding, self-sufficient, and hardworking. Even as federal and state laws privileged big business, government has made efforts to perpetuate the small firm and encourage entrepreneurialism—and its perceived moral effects—on a small scale. The formation of the Small Business Administration in 1953 emerged out of this conflicted view.[4] Similarly, American artisanal culture, which emphasized the central community role of the skilled craftsman, remains crucial to the moral orientations of American working-class men. Michele Lamont's interviews with working-class and managerial-class men in the 1990s reveal significant differences in moral outlook. While working-class men emphasize straightforwardness, service to community, and protection of family as evidence of strong moral character, managerial-class men report "self actualization and conflict avoidance."[5] The American ideal of the small business person encompasses all of these markers of character, thus becoming a powerful metaphor for the American work ethic.[6] The entrepreneurial exhibit, created by workers to explain their work, is a critical medium through which Americans comment on class structure and the increasingly bureaucratized nature of the contemporary workplace.

The growth of America's corporations means that artisanal models of work are few and far between, replaced by models that emphasize worker mobility over job stability.[7] Workers use the entrepreneurial exhibition to assert control over their roles as citizens in a labor community. In so doing, they provide a moral critique of corporatism and its effect on community life. While the entrepreneurial exhibit is more common for professions that were (or still are) traditionally trade-focused like printing or plumbing, or public service professions like firefighting or teaching, other professions currently associated with big business—like journalism or funeral directing—have also produced exhibits in the entrepreneurial style, perhaps in attempts to regain lost moral ground. People in professions considered less than genteel like freak-show workers or strippers have used the entrepreneurial exhibit to tell their histories in a way that helps visitors make personal connections to workers. Entrepreneurial exhibits use history to promote the trade or profession, train students, articulate the craft's effect on cultural heritage, and provide role models. Like the community exhibit, the entrepreneurial exhibit represents the perspective of a community group—in this case, communities of workers. The entrepreneurial exhibit's focus on work, hands-on experiences, and spatial proximity to small business or office produces reactions in visitors that are different from those evoked by the community exhibit. Visitors view the exhibit in the moral terms used to define the small business person's role in the community. A worker, whether service worker or small business owner, as represented by the exhibit and as perceived by visitors, is a figure that holds together the broader community. This validates the work ethic as social glue and leads both visitors and curators to experience the exhibit in those terms. The interpretive techniques of these exhibitions, primarily face-to-face conversation and hands-on experiential learning, reflect this dynamic.

While the emphasis on the dignity of work and the face-to-face approach to teaching are common to entrepreneurial exhibits, their places on the political spectrum vary widely. They promote varying ideas about gender, race, immigration, war, and sexuality, offering interpretation of history for almost any combination of political views. On work, however, there is only one message, whether implicit or explicit: "what we do matters—to everyone."

TRAINING FOR PROFESSIONAL MEMBERSHIP

Part of training students for a new field means giving them the history of the craft. Future pharmacists, teachers, bartenders, plumbers, firefighters, and nurses, for example, often begin their studies not with the latest knowledge or practices, but with those of the past. Exhibitions are vital tools for this pedagogy. The Chicago area alone has history museums devoted to surgeons, actors, sailors, and teachers. While many exhibits on specific types of work are in stand-alone museums, others are built into more formal instructional areas. The Blackwell History of Education Museum, what journalist Jennifer Olvera calls a "haven for potential teachers," features historic textbooks, schoolroom re-creations, and a sizable collection of instructional technologies. It is located on the campus of Northern Illinois University in DeKalb, where it is easily accessible to teachers in training.[8] The Funeral Institute of Northeast Mortuary College keeps a museum room close to its classrooms.[9] The Texas Pharmacy Museum is in the basement of the Texas Tech School of Pharmacy.[10] In 2006, the Kentucky Nurses Association Chapter 8, a professional organization serving six counties, curated and mounted a traveling exhibition, installed first in the lobby of Independence Bank in Owensboro, Kentucky. Chronicling over one hundred years of nursing history, the exhibit included uniforms, equipment, and an early twentieth-century ad promoting nursing school that proclaimed "Be a Nurse—The Profession With a Future."[11]

Workers facing futures less certain than those of nurses—like freak-show performers or burlesque dancers—use the exhibition medium to explain their crafts. Johnny Fox's Freakatorium: El Museo Loco, located in Manhattan from 1999 to 2005, featured a collection of oddities including Victorian taxidermy, freak-show posters, Tom Thumb's clothes and Sammy Davis Jr.'s glass eye. Run by sword swallower Johnny Fox, it also served as a booking agency for freak show workers. The Freakatorium's web site offered "The Peerless Prodigies and Performers of the Freakatorium's booking services featuring: Little people, contortionists, fairies, ballerinas, exotic musicians, snake dancers, stiltwalkers, sword swallowers and fire eaters. Rest assured your guests will have a spectacular evening from the moment they walk in the door until the fat lady sings!"[12] Dixie Evans, burlesque dancer turned curator, ran Exotic World/Burlesque Hall of Fame, originally of Helendale, California, but now in the process of establishment in Las Vegas, Nevada. Evans notes that strippers today differ markedly from those of the past: "They come out and immediately get down and risqué. In our era you came out in full dress, with a gorgeous wardrobe and music and you wound up with a shake number." She is also motivated by public neglect of burlesque dance, noting that "burlesque has not been covered professionally in our history books. They want to sweep it under the carpet and pretend it didn't exist. . . . Well, it did exist, and it existed in a big way. This was entertainment that was affordable to the working class. For twenty-five cents they could go and see a great show."[13] The museum hosted an annual reunion where strippers of past and present converse and perform. Evans has played a role in the revitalization of burlesque; in 2002 she was an honored guest at Tease-O-Rama, a burlesque convention featuring young performers reviving the old traditions by studying features of past performances.[14]

Professions that get respect in contemporary society sponsor exhibits that explore how far they have come from past practices and how contemporary practices may be improved by studying the past. The Country Doctor Museum exhibits in Bailey, North Carolina, function to both inspire and horrify visitors. Founded in 1967 by a group of women (three of them physicians), the museum is currently operated by Laupus Library of East Carolina University. Exhibits include an apothecary shop, an examining room, and displays on nursing and transportation. ECU's purpose in acquiring the museum was to provide inspiration for contemporary students in the medical field; it, according to Dr. Michael Lewis, vice chancellor for health sciences, "is a tribute to those who have served the community. . . .

As we educate physicians, this museum is a chance to demonstrate practices that have withstood the test of time—trust, compassion, caring."[15] Visitors, however, tend to focus on practices that are obsolete, especially if they are horrifying. "Take a deep breath before your enter" warned one journalist, recounting her visit in 2001.[16] A more recent visit yielded the following description:

> Relief is what you feel after a visit to the Country Doctor Museum in Bailey. You're relieved, mainly, to be a citizen of our modern age. Whatever horror the dental chair might visit upon you, it's nothing so ghastly as the tooth key that managed to combine a corkscrew apparatus with pliers that, in the hands of a country doctor 100 years ago, yanked rotting molars. "It usually crushed the tooth in the process," program and event coordinator Jennie Schindler calmly notes. Oh. Dear. God.[17]

This account, as well as others that included horror, also included respect for country doctors, for the reasons identified by Dr. Lewis. A 2005 article titled "Sawbones Central" ended with a genuine appreciation of the profession:

> The chief feeling engendered by the museum, though, isn't amusement or horror at this evidence of primitive and mostly misguided attempts to fix up folks—but an unabashed gratitude that doctors did as much as they did while knowing so little. There's a touching naïveté about these devices and potions. People's sufferings were taken seriously.[18]

Chicago's International Museum of Surgical Science features exhibits not only on the gory history of surgery, but also art shows that directly confront visitors' squeamishness, such as an exhibition of Laura Splan's drawings in her own blood. Viewer reactions move "between seduction and repulsion, comfort and alienation," reports Splan. The show fits in with the museum's historical collections, what one journalist called the "usual fare of iron lungs and Civil War amputation instruments."[19] The museum has an almost cult status as an institution outside the gentility of contemporary museum practices, a status one journalist said made it "a perennial favorite in the pantheon of offbeat Chicago sites." Even its label choices reflect this:

> In an era when most museum exhibits are ultra-slick endeavors, assembled by teams of academics and funded by multinational corporations, the surgical museum is endearingly rustic, almost crude, in a cobbled-together way, between rough stone statues in its Hall of Immortals, and the haphazard jumble of displays, identified haltingly with handmade labels, all skewed and fading.
> But the folksiness of the place also contributes to its chamber-of-horrors feel, the way the serenity of a town in a Stephen King novel underlines the nightmares building below the surface.[20]

Education on medical topics is always fraught with emotion, but exhibits in smaller, less "ultra-slick" museums heighten the emotional response. The intimacy of exhibits in the Country Doctor Museum and the International Museum of Surgical Science inspires strong visitor reactions and ultimately leads some to heightened respect for medical practitioners.

The Glore Psychiatric Museum in St. Joseph, Missouri, also operates on visitors' feelings of horror of the past. It is also a source for public dialogue about treatment for mental illnesses and reflects the use of the past for validating or shaping present values or even policy. Founded by St. Joseph State Hospital retiree George Glore, the museum houses artifacts related to historic "treatments," usually gruesome enough to be evoked by those arguing for better care for present sufferers of mental illness. These include a re-creation of a wheel treadmill on which patients were forced to run for long periods, a chair and chains in which patients would be physically restrained for months or years, 1,446 items removed from the digestive tract of a patient, lobotomy instruments, and 100,000 cigarette packs collected by a patient who thought he could turn them in for a new wheelchair.[21] A news story covering hospital states and outpatient services for the mentally ill starts with an example featured in the Glore exhibits: a man who spent seventy-two years in St. Joseph State Hospital.[22]

Figure 4.1.   Display of items removed from a patient's digestive tract, Glore Psychiatric Museum. (Photo courtesy of The St. Joseph Museums, Inc., St. Joseph, Missouri.)

A group arguing for research on and preservation of State Hospital grave-yards identified the text on a patient's headstone, leading the reporter to ponder the quality of the patient's life: "One can only guess at the primitive 'treatments' this 34-year-old woman endured before she died. Or you don't have to guess if you view the collection of macabre instruments in the psychiatric museum that St. Joseph's mental hospital has become."[23] One parent brought her twelve- and ten-year-old sons because "I wanted my kids to know how far we've come, and how cruelly we used to treat people." Apparently, the boys got the point; one of them "almost got sick looking at the displays" while the other noted the exhibits showed practices that were "all wrong."[24] George Glore, now retired from the museum, articulated the exhibit's interpretive approach in terms of moral improvement: "We really can't have a good appreciation of the strides we've made if we don't look at the atrocities of the past." He also looked to expand sections on patient art to offer visitors more than "the macabre."[25]

This kind of effort at remembering also marks exhibits at military museums. These are both interpretive and commemorative, but their main point is to explain soldiering from the point of view of soldiers. Exhibits at the 82nd Airborne Division War Memorial Museum and the JFK Special Warfare Museum, both in North Carolina, educate soldiers about sacrifice. Visited primarily by soldiers of the past and present, the JFK Special Warfare Museum draws around 64,000 visitors per year. "If the general public comes and likes what we have, that's icing on the cake," museum director Roxanne Merritt explained. Bob Anzuoni of the 82nd Airborne Museum noted "most people don't know we're Army. Our mission is to train soldiers as well."[26] Nonsoldiers react with a new respect for troops. Journalist Lynn Setzer presented an outsider visitor experience in 2001: "Stepping inside the JFK Special Warfare Museum, I had no clear idea of what to expect. What constituted 'special warfare,' I wondered. Quickly, however, the picture came into focus." Setzer described the exhibition narrative through late nineteenth-century Indian Scouts, through the World Wars and up to Vietnam, where she paused at a re-creation of a POW camp: "The re-created living conditions of a POW camp will put a lump in your throat, as will the homemade playing cards made by Sgt. Canny Pitzer from old shoe boxes. The five years' worth of scores, neatly written on a small piece of paper, adds poignancy to what you see."[27] This visitor's transition from perplexity to sympathy is the result of an interpretive approach that mixes memorial with job training: it gives reason for "doing what we do."

Some exhibits are so strongly identified with the professional culture that they alienate visitors from outside the field. A recent visitor to the National Border Patrol Museum (El Paso, Texas), in a contribution to the web magazine *Hyphen: Asian America Unabridged*, reported surprise at the even tone of the interpretation: it addressed some of the economic reasons for immigration and recognized the complexity of immigration regulation in the United States. A single object brought about a change in this visitor's reaction to the exhibits: a photograph of guards at the Tule Lake Internment Camp in a section on patrol guard duty during war time:

> I felt as though this picture being framed on the wall of the National Border Patrol Museum was celebrating the duty of these soldiers whose job was a huge mistake. I guess it was the total lack of context that bothered me the most. I don't know what I wanted: A sign next to this photograph explaining how Japanese internment was one of the most heinous things that happened in American history? A section of the museum talking about NAFTA and global-ization and how the U.S. depends on illegal labor? Perhaps they can remove the entire wall of sharp shooting prizes that covers most of the back wall and make room for some of my ideas.[28]

This blogger's response has not been the only public criticism of the Border Patrol Museum. In 1989, a visitor complained about a t-shirt in the gift shop with "a grinning Mexican whose foot is thrust through a wire fence" under the universal circle-slash symbol for "no." After a story in the El Paso Times and complaints to the museum, the museum's director pulled the shirts from the gift shop.[29]

These interactions result not just from differences in political opinion. The purpose of the entrepreneurial exhibit, when employed as part of pro-fessional training, is to define who belongs to a craft or professional group and who does not. The training exhibition defines professional culture, whether by sacrifice, as in the Special Warfare exhibits, or by irreverence, as in the Freakatorium displays. The political overtones (or undertones) emerge from delineation of professional subculture.

CRAFT AND THE "WAY OF LIFE"

Some entrepreneurial exhibits function not only to teach visitors about a profession but also to evoke a community life governed by that trade but extended to nonmembers. Farm museums exemplify this the most, for while their purpose is to explain farming, they also emphasize idea of rural life off the farm proper. While most farm museums could not be termed "small museums" by their square footage, their professional staff numbers are comparable to museums with less exhibition space; they rely heavily on volunteers. Exhibits are likely to address "farm life" as a cultural and social orientation than farming as a profession. This, according to both those run-ning farm museums and those visiting them, is their primary appeal.

The mission of the Washington County Farm Museum, open from May to October on the county's fairgrounds, is "to cultivate an appreciation for agriculture by educating visitors about our rural heritage." In addition to displays of equipment and outbuildings related to "dairying, poultry, potatoes, crop production and ice harvesting," the museum offers a re-created country school to show visitors some of life away from the day-to-day chores of the farm. Motivations for the museum are also presentist; it can "muster support for local farmers and their land by educating visitors about the region's agricultural heritage." One assemblyman pointed out that its appeal could be profitable as well: "It's an education process for people who don't come from the farm community. It's extremely interesting and we might be able to make some money out of it to boot."[30]

The appeal of the farm museum is largely governed by its experiential possibilities. The Pioneer Farm Museum in Eatonville, Washington, hosted fifth graders and their parents for a night on the farm, which ended when they "arose at 6, ate johnnycakes—fried biscuits they made in class to duplicate a pioneer staple—and did barn chores such as milking goats, catching chickens and spinning wool."[31] Chicagoan Jeanne Zasadil paid sixty dollars to learn how to drive oxen at the Garfield Farm Museum: "I know not many people are into manure and mud, but it's fun."[32] In addition to opportunities to do laundry and other chores using methods and equipment resembling those of the 1770s, visitors to Claude Moore Colonial Farm can sign up for the more extensive farm skills program, "a workshop that offers hands-on experience for all sorts of Colonial skills and games."[33] For some, training at farm museums is the first step in a lifelong hobby, or even a new trade, as blacksmith Randy McDaniel demonstrates. In 1973 he paid two dollars to take a blacksmithing course at a farm museum near his Maryland home. The course inspired him to take more classes. By 2002 he ran Dragonfly Enterprises, a successful iron forge, and had published a book on blacksmithing.[34]

Foci on mechanical ability as the central feature in a unique way of life are not exclusive to farm museums. Da Yoopers Tourist Trap and Museum in Ishpeming, Michigan, created by Jim "Hoolie" DeCaire and his musical group Da Yoopers, includes an exhibit that explains and celebrates Yooper innovation and adaptation to a harsh climate and limited resources. While not technically about a trade, the exhibit "Yooper Innovation" is about skill and its centrality to cultural practice. The museum is a collection of objects created by residents of the Upper Peninsula of Michigan ("Yoopers"), usually out of scrap materials and in response to the demands of the harsh weather. The objects, built between the 1890s and the 1960s, are among mineral displays, dioramas about deer camps and outhouses, and large metalwork art with U.P. themes, including the obligatory giant mosquito reference and the world's largest operating chainsaw. Each object's label begins with "Yooper Innovation." The museum is so irreverent toward exhibit standards and guidelines that it operates in the realm of parody.

DeCaire, the self-described "Head Guy," reports that everything about his museum is informed by the Yooper sense of humor. Ishpeming is a city whose past is rooted in extraction industries supported by a primarily immigrant population. Workers from Europe came to the area in the nineteenth century to work in iron mines and lumber camps. Isolated by harsh climate, the current resident population is high in second- and third-generation Americans. As one reporter summed up the local culture, "the town is sports-crazy, hunting happy and tough as nails, with a population descended from Cornish, Finnish and Italian immigrants who could put up with the rigors of iron mines and, later, their closings. Residents think they're part of Wisconsin and that they suffer the world's longest winter and heaviest snowfalls, and they're almost right on all counts."[35] While "Yooper Innovation" has many exhibition practices that are irreverent, such as human models made with old clothes, Halloween masks, and a variety of taxidermied animals, the curatorial voice is one that most reflects the creators' conception of visitors. The first sign the visitor encounters reads "Welcome to Yooperland. Relax. Enjoy. Spend all your cash. But please don't move up here." It was signed by the "Head Guy." The curatorial voice assumes that the visitor is a tourist with little knowledge of Upper Peninsula culture and little skill in adapting to its harsh climate. The voice on the labels is the stereotypical "Yooper Guy": ironic, lax with the rules of standard English grammar, and, of course, knowledgeable about and skilled with machinery. The label for the two snowmachines adapted with wheels best exemplified this curatorial voice: "Yooper Innovation. A Sno-Cicle, invented by Brian Katayamaki. Why you ask? So a Yooper guy can keep riding his snowmachine for the one month we ain't got no snow. What you tink you stooge ball?"[36]

A curatorial voice that addresses the visitor as a "stooge ball" is definitely not an approach advocated by best practices literature on visitor services. Visitors, however, did not seem to mind at all. They took their time through the exhibit, read labels aloud, and discussed the interpretation (all markers of effective exhibition technique) even though the temperature hovered around fifty—in early August—and the rain came down at a 45-degree angle. In addition, interviews with visitors yielded an interesting phenomenon: former Yoopers bringing their non-Yooper spouses to explain their Upper Peninsula identities. Two visitor groups out of a twenty-six group sample identified this as the main goal of their visit. DeCaire reports that one of the reasons for the success of the museum is that the area's economic hard times have forced some residents to look elsewhere for work; what keeps them from being homesick is a visit to the museum or its website, authored by DeCaire's son Jesse. Not all Yoopers were pleased, however. DeCaire reports that the local Chamber of Commerce tried to downplay the success of the museum, queasy about the image of Yoopers as 24-hour-a-day jokers and tinkerers. As DeCaire puts it, "They think

Figure 4.2. Objects attesting to mechanical ability to adapt: Da Sno-Cicle. Many objects in Yooper Innovation were actually used. Others are just tall tales in 3D. The curator does not reveal which is which. (Da Yoopers Tourist Trap, Ishpeming, Michigan, 2005. Photo by author.)

we're Yooper hillbillies."[37] Likewise, the museum's assertion that Yoopers are defined by region, mechanical ability, and sense of humor is a way to maintain local control over local identity. One recent trend in cultural display is for local groups to hire heritage professionals who come in from outside the community, "harvest" heritage resources like material artifacts and oral histories, and produce exhibits in consultation with locals.[38] The DeCaires' homemade approach to exhibition represents a backlash against such conventions of professional heritage exhibition. It is also a reaction against a more general outsider view of Yoopers. Hoolie DeCaire cites the movie *Escanaba in Da Moonlight,* with its depiction of Yoopers in deerskin pants, as a particularly egregious appropriation of identity and emphasizes the importance of not taking identity too seriously.[39] This insistence on local control of identity finds a great deal of support from visitors, especially visitors from the Upper Peninsula. One summed it up succinctly by saying "The U.P. people are represented here."[40]

Da Yoopers' "Yooper Innovation" is part of a larger effort to use humor to benefit the community, an effort local health authorities find useful. Ray Sharp of the Western Upper Peninsula District Health Department used Da Yoopers' community reputation to increase enrollment in MIChild and Healthy Kids, programs aimed at responding to the health needs of under- or uninsured children. Sharp arranged displays featuring Da Yoopers and including program enrollment forms to be installed in gas stations in the area. "Say Ya to Affordable Health Care" was the tag line accompanying the displays. Public service announcements recorded by Da Yoopers reinforced the message and enrollment in the program increased. Sharp credited success of the effort to the popularity of Da Yoopers—especially their appeal to low-income families: "We always talk about collaboration, but we usually only collaborate with the same people."[41] The Health Department's unconventional approach reflected significant understanding of local culture and Da Yoopers' role in it.

Exhibits that emphasize hands-on skills appeal to visitors' experiential learning needs. While history museums have always attracted those with a standing commitment to antimodernism, exhibits with opportunities to use one's body as people have done in the past are even more appealing during a digital revolution. Amidst what Charlie Gere has called "the whole panoply of virtual simulacra, instantaneous communication, ubiquitous media and global connectivity that constitutes much of our contemporary experience,"[42] activities like making johnnycakes or driving oxen, which require more physical engagement and sensual opportunity, become the exotic, sensory experiences for those whose access to modern technologies is a fait accompli.

CRAFT AND CONVERSATION

While some entrepreneurial exhibits exist to explain a profession's practices to outsiders, imbue a sense of history to new practitioners, attach certain skills to certain cultures, or provide temporary relief from the dominance of the virtual, other entrepreneurial exhibitions provide a much broader scope, provoking thought on issues of social justice and the meaning of community. These exhibits depend on individual curators' abilities to bring visitors from a focus on artifacts to a focus on issues, and these abilities emerge from skill combinations (mainly craft and social skills) but also to a large degree on sheer personality.

The Olde Mill House Printing Museum, Gallery, and Café offers one example of this type of entrepreneurial exhibit, and nothing exemplifies this better than one incident that marked its beginnings. Jim Anderson, described by one journalist as "self-made printer, curator, jazz musician, home-spun philosopher and father,"[43] was in the process of creating his Olde Mill House Printing Museum in the small fishing village of Old Homosassa, Florida in 1995—moving around heavy printing presses, fine-tuning machinery—when he heard a knock on the door. He knew, as one of the few African Americans who had moved to the predominantly white town, that he was visible in the community already, but he had yet to find out exactly how his presence was felt. Surprised at having visitors to a museum that hadn't even opened, he answered the door. To his even greater surprise, he found three white men swaying from the effect of drink. He relates the encounter:

> "Can I help you?"
> "We've come over here to beat your ass, man."
> So there's three of them standing there, right. And my vision goes past them at the tavern and everybody's out there looking . . . . They're all looking . . . .
> "Well, it's going to take all three of you guys to whup my ass?"
> And they looked at each other kind of. And I says "I tell you what. Tell you what. Before this ass whupping, come inside, and let's talk." And sure enough, they all three came inside . . . and they started looking at all the things.[44]

As Mr. Anderson tells it, the three drew conclusions about the curator's strength from his ability to move printing presses by himself (and probably from his muscular appearance as well). Furthermore, they became interested in the machines themselves: how they worked, who used them, how they were maintained. Anderson gave them a brief tour, and they started to forget their original reason for coming to the museum. By the time he finished the tour, the three exited the front door, disappointing the audience looking out the bar window across the street, the group expecting to get a front row seat to some racially motivated violence. While this was Mr. Anderson's most dramatic encounter with racism in his museum, it certainly has not been his only. An amazing communicator, this curator attracts people with diverse ideas about race, doing much to talk people out of their sometimes long-held misperceptions about African Americans.[45] He attributes his visitors' changed ideas to the fact that his museum's mission is about communication and that "Old things can break down barriers."[46] He also notes that while artifacts may bring strangers together, it is up to the individuals to communicate. Like other small museums around the country, the Olde Mill House Printing Museum brings strangers together to talk, often about race, ethnicity, culture, identity, and inequality. They employ communication models that are different from larger, more mainstream museums. These small museums rely on the abilities of their curators to communicate face-to-face with visitors, a communication facilitated by intimate multiuse exhibition spaces that encourage informal conversation. Summative evaluation surveys indicate that visitors in these settings respond positively to this intimacy and demonstrate significant receptivity to conversation outside their visitor groups.[47]

Small museums are more personality-driven than larger museums, and visitors report that curator personality is key to maintaining their interest. Several visitors to the Printing Museum attributed its success to the outgoing personality of its creator: people come to the museum to learn not just about the history of printing, but to learn about Mr. Anderson the printer.

One visitor reported "Talking to Jim helps you learn about the artifacts, which doesn't happen in a lot of museums. Jim breathes life into these artifacts. His personal experience and reverence for this old equipment makes a bigger impact. I like the eccentric quality of this place—the combination of art, history, and food. It is Jim's personality brought to life."[48]

The museum's focus on communication emphasizes individual responsibility in identity creation. As a printer himself, he knows much about the possibilities and limits of print communication. The digital age was his inspiration for creating the printing museum. He observed the changes in the trade he had been in since he was a teenager and took on the role of saving and explaining the old methods of printing. His collections include inked blocks, iron hand letterpresses, and platen letterpresses, all operational. His desire to bring his printing business from Tampa and create the museum in Old Homosassa was inspired in part by the presence of the sugar mill ruins in this small Florida town. Descended from cane workers, Mr. Anderson identifies strongly with Florida's African American past. He blends these interests in his museum and can move smoothly from talking about printing press technology to identity. He is highly sensitive to visitor individuality. He begins each tour with a word from an antique dictionary; he chooses this word based on his visitors' interests, which he discusses before the tour. Each tour stresses human ability to communicate, which is what he sees as the ultimate message of the artifacts.

The fact that the Olde Mill House Printing Museum fronts Anderson's printing company Gemini Graphics is key to understanding the curator's highly developed conversational skills. A printer since his teens, Anderson has been a small business owner for most of his adult life. While his wife and business partner kept books and managed much of the behind the scenes work, Anderson brought in business through personal contacts. When the business grew to support twelve employees, the Andersons reached a crossroads: they either had to increase business or cut back. They decided that keeping the business small would effect a welcome lifestyle change. They focused on keeping the business of a few key customers and moved Gemini Graphics to the small fishing village of Old Homosassa, north of Tampa. As a part of that move, Anderson started to collect obsolete printing equipment, and the museum side of the business began to grow. As word of his museum spread through the local tourist council, tour groups started coming in. Anderson's tours—combinations of printing history, philosophy, informal conversation and maybe even a blues tune—appeal to locals and tourists alike:

> This kind of blew me away a little bit—even though people were coming in to see the print shop, a few people were coming in to see that *guy* . . . . I really didn't want it to be this way. I don't want you to come to see me, I wanted you

to come and see what I'm about, my trade. I guess people got inquisitive about me to a degree . . . . Well anyway, it worked out ok, and the groups started coming through.[49]

Anderson is keenly aware that as an African American man in a predominantly white town he is a visible figure, possibly a divisive one. He is, however, quite open in claiming identity based on the town itself; the "Olde Mill House" in his museum's name is from its proximity to the ruins of the sugar mill attached to the Yulee plantation operating in the area before the Civil War: "When those thousand slaves were here and those Union soldiers came and disbanded Yulee's plantation, where did they go? Where did those slaves go? In my lineage."[50] With visitors, Anderson will gladly talk about the history of slavery and what this history means to him personally. Such conversations have had profound effects on individuals and have assisted some in unlearning long-held racist beliefs. Anderson takes real communication seriously, and emphasizes listening as well as talking. First, however, social boundaries among individuals must be crossed, and this is where he says the history of a trade can do that. Work is common ground, but printing is not. The artifacts of his trade enable the first conversation:

That old press right there, no other way that person may have came to me, but that press brought him to the conversation that we're having, know what I'm saying? I'm just saying, a person may not come toward you for the sake of being who you are on a physical level, but if there's something old here, it's going to break the tension, and now we can communicate. Because they're interested in that, and they don't know that much about it, but I do, I know something about that, so that's going to bring us together. You know, for the sake of my knowledge of that and you're not having that knowledge. That is what I'm speaking about. Old things can break down barriers to communicate.[51]

Anderson's we're-here-together-let's-talk approach to curation is one that emphasizes the exhibition's position between public and private. While the exhibition is a public place, the interpretation is private and individualized. It is highly personal and derivative from experiential authority.

Anderson has expanded upon his entrepreneurial exhibit to add other types to the museum. He added a Cuban sandwich restaurant where visitors could stay for lunch. This has become as popular as the museum. The restaurant is decorated with a diversity of objects and artifacts, including a Model T, works by local photographers and painters, a sign that washed up in a hurricane, and printing artifacts. The effect is to evoke a general respect for the past as well as interest in the collector.

Anderson has also begun to create another exhibition in a small building behind the restaurant. When the nearby Atlanta Fishing Club wanted to move its old chauffeur's cabin, Anderson agreed to take it to his property.

In the late nineteenth and early twentieth century, wealthy white business-men came from Atlanta to Old Homosassa to fish; their chauffeurs stayed on site in the cabin now in Anderson's possession. Some of the drivers left their marks on the wall: a name, a date, place of origin. Some left more information, providing insight into the rather undocumented lives of these men. Ebenezer Williams of Macon, Georgia, visited in 1944 and again in 1946. On his first visit he left the comment: "You can have it boys because I don't want it and wouldn't have it. Plenty of risk." He continued the theme in 1946: "Still plenty of risk. As usual plenty to eat. Many miles from nowhere. Here we stay 5 days." Anderson tells visitors that these young African American drivers felt isolated, and conjectures the "risk" Williams was not willing to take was probably sex with white servant girls. Anderson is currently preparing the cabin for public view, and uses the porch in his blues festival. Anderson wrote a song about Ebenezer Williams's lonely visits to the cabin, a tune he plans to perform on the site. Even in his plans for developing this local history exhibit, his perspective is still significantly informed by the logic of entrepreneurial exhibition. It was, after all, Eb-enezer Williams's role as worker that brought him to Old Homosassa and Jim Anderson's brief stint as a chauffeur that made him identify with the historic figure in the first place.[52]

The entrepreneurial exhibition is the result of several crosscurrents in American society and culture. The tradition of the small business, with its owner as model citizen and scion of community and its spaces dominated by informal conversation and close proximity, guides the curation and gal-lery opportunities. As the globalized economy gives the impression that one's work is not place-based, the entrepreneurial exhibition asserts the real effects one's work has on the community. For visitors, the entrepreneurial exhibit provides a place for hands-on experiences, informal face-to-face conversations, and other activities that provide reprieve from interactions with digital technologies. While the entrepreneurial exhibit could be seen as a backlash against the bureaucracy and technology of contemporary life, it is ultimately these that ensure its existence. Its nostalgia for an artisanal life brings visitors to the doors of museums with entrepreneurial exhibits. Visitors, saturated in virtual media and overwhelmed with bureaucracy, find comfort in the sometimes intense experiences of past work and the community that emerged from those work experiences.

5

Vernacular Exhibition and the Business of History

Ivar's Acres of Clams in Seattle, Washington, is a restaurant that tells local history through the biography of its founder, or "Flounder," as the employee orientation manual states, the colorful Ivar Haglund. A large photo of Ivar Haglund greets the visitor from behind the host's stand. The dining area includes nautical artifacts and photos of historic Seattle, a display named "Ivar's Waterfront Walking Tour." The introductory label explains the development of the exhibit and indicates the connectedness between Ivar, Seattle, and food:

> Ivar Haglund chose most of these photographs while sipping clam nectar and swallowing oysters during lunch . . . . Another old salt and Ivar's long time friend, Jim Faber often joined him, and together they would play the game of "Name that Picture." While I pulled these photographs from my bag and set them upright on the table they would respond. Some scenes would trigger loud guffaws, others meaningful murmurs, and many more would call up an old story.
>
> We might have kept up meeting like that, consuming gallons of Viking Soup, downing dozens of Olympic oysters, and thumbing through old photos for many more months of lunches, but Ivar unexpectedly left us for the Captain's Table in the Sky.[1]

Placemats at Ivar's Acres of Clams continue the interpretation of Seattle and the restaurant's founder, providing visual documentation of Haglund's exploits from the founding of the restaurant in 1946 until his death in 1985. Staff receive training in this history; the training manual explains that "it is important that you know as much as possible about the origins of our company. As you work your shift you will get many questions from our guests about various things concerning Ivar's." The manual proceeds with a brief history of Haglund's background as a singer and how his aquarium business led to the founding of the restaurant. Haglund was voted "The Person Who Best Exemplified Seattle."[2] The historical interpretation at Ivar's demonstrates the connectedness between consumption, history, individuality, and place. In this way it is typical of vernacular exhibitions in the United States. This type of exhibition allows people to discuss heritage without breaking from daily activities: working, eating, getting a haircut, drinking. The interpretation is developed in similar ways to professional museums: first content is researched (albeit not to academic standards) and organized, then staff receives training in this history so that they can respond to customers' questions. Vernacular exhibition content delivery is geared toward both those from the community or elsewhere, and functions as a way for insiders and outsiders to exchange information about the past.

Vernacular exhibitions cross boundaries between education and business. Large not-for-profit educational institutions carefully distinguish between educational and business functions, most notably that businesses attached to museums "pay the bills" so that education can occur.[3] The logic of vernacular exhibitions is neither governed nor troubled by this dichotomy. Display of historic material is part of doing business, part of creating an

Figure 5.1. The menu at Ivar's asserts the connection between food and local history. (Courtesy of Ivar's, Seattle, Washington, February 2005.)

atmosphere that evokes emotional connections and responses, a common practice for both small enterprises and large corporations. National chain restaurants use vernacular exhibition to assert the local authenticity of the business. McDonald's, Cracker Barrel, and Bennigan's are examples of large businesses employing local history to claim a role in the community. Some-times the efforts are rather curious, such as a display of snowshoes in a central North Carolina Cracker Barrel, and are sometimes rather transparent, given their dependence on reproductions. The corporate effort to re-create this historical intimacy in chain restaurants and other venues has been criticized because the history is employed for "atmosphere" by people without connections to the community. Jerry Herron, in *AfterCulture: Detroit and the Humiliation of History,* asserts that corporately produced history-as-marketing often leads to a sanitized version of the past, a version that is divorced from the problems of the present. He uses the example of Greektown in Detroit, where middle-class visitors come to Greektown to experience the "authentic" working-class, ethnic urban neighborhood of the past. But security guards and local ordinances keep the legacy of that past—any evidence of crime or crumbling infrastructure—out of Greektown. Herron asserts such practices keep us from reflecting on history's lessons.[4] Corporate and franchise attempts at local credibility, while technically vernacular exhibition, are not the primary focus of this chapter because they have been researched and designed by professionals from without the community. Restaurant design firms focus on the goal of national sameness, even though restaurants may be themed with local artifacts.[5]

Vernacular exhibition differs from academic, corporate, community, and entrepreneurial exhibition in that neither the curator nor the visitor break from the activities of daily life in order to experience the display. This makes a profound difference in visitors' ideas about the past. In a more traditional exhibition, visitors see the past as something to be learned; in a vernacular exhibition, visitors see the past as something to be felt or even experienced. The process is helped by the physical presence of the curator, usually the business owner, who is not only highly involved in the business, but a central figure in the community. Like entrepreneurial exhibits, vernacular exhibits rely heavily on face-to-face conversations between curators and visitors, but also among visitors. Unlike entrepreneurial or indigenous exhibits, they rely on the visitor's status as a consumer of goods and services other than the exhibition. Vernacular exhibition curators rely on their displays to express their personal views to customers, creating an intimacy that supports the business by encouraging the visitor to make personal connections with the business. In this way, private history told in public is inextricably linked with the processes of production and consumption. Its results, however, go beyond simple economic life and sometimes translate to direct political action.

THE ROOTS OF VERNACULAR EXHIBITION

Themed artifact displays outside the direction and space of the museum have their roots in the development of restaurants in the early twentieth century. As local businesses responded to the food and beverage needs of automobile travelers, their customer base changed from local to a mix of local and national. Historians have shown how automobility created major changes in business practices as well as the eating habits of Americans, giving a boost to both franchising and eating out. By the 1930s, consumers came to desire both predictability, which spawned the increasing use of the franchise, and "atmosphere," a sense that one is indeed in a place apart from one's own.[6] Early versions of Kentucky Fried Chicken—Sanders Courts in Corbin, Kentucky—used spinning wheels, hearths, and muskets to evoke an early-American period, while Knott's Berry Farm created a "Wild West" theme park near its restaurant.[7] Over the 1940s and 50s, as fast food chains focused on each restaurant looking the same, some restaurants sought to evoke the uniqueness of place, and used artifacts to decorate, like Victoria Station in San Francisco, founded in 1969 to evoke the feeling of being in a train station.[8] The success of the Hard Rock Café in London, opening in that same year with its displays of rock-n-roll artifacts, emphasized that the time had come for nostalgia theming.[9]

The sports bar represents the newest and one of the most common forms of vernacular exhibition and the increase in consumer demand for "experience" commodities. It came to be known in its present form with the opening of Champions in Washington, D.C., in 1983, and it was the presence of memorabilia and its focus on female patronage that set it apart.[10] Mike O'Harro and Joe Desmond, former owners of Gentlemen's II, a singles bar, and Tramp's, a disco, wanted to create a singles bar with a theme more lasting than disco, and set upon sports. O'Harro remembered the evolution of the concept as such:

> Mine was not the first sports bar . . . . Jack Dempsey had a bar in the forties. There were others: bars where a bunch of fat former high school football players would watch a little black and white TV . . . . Having been in the singles bar business, I wanted to create a place where women could say they were going to watch the game, not just to meet guys.[11]

O'Harro's soon-to-be notorious attitude toward women was more objectifying and less egalitarian,[12] but women flocked to Champions. The bar courted female clientele with a dance floor, better-than-average meals, and a space that was "light and airy," as opposed to the "dark rat hole" feeling of other bars.[13]

While the presence of single ladies set the bar apart, so did its décor: memorabilia, lots of it. Eight months after Champions' opening, journalist Jeffrey Yorke provided a description of the use of artifacts in the bar:

> Every inch of the décor is 20th century jock—even the alley is carpeted with artificial turf once used in Byrd Stadium's end zone. Nearly every type of athletic equipment used over the past 75 years either hangs from, or is bolted to, the walls. A 1933 sprint car, the kind raced at the Brickyard, sits on a pedestal above the doorway. And what other bar in town would dare park an original 1948 Whizzer motorcycle on the ledge above the steps? Below the bike hangs a framed front page declaring the Redskins Super Bowl champions....You'll find a sulky from a Rosecroft, a Sammy Baugh movie poster, an original sign from Old Griffith Stadium, one of Frank Howard's bats, a pair of Moses Mallone sneakers . . . and uniforms worn by Pete Wysocki of the Redskins, Tom Mack of the Rams, Phil Chenier and Mitch Kupchak of the Bullets, and Kermit Washington's jersey from American University.[14]

Yorke completed his description of the artifactual decadence of Champions by noting how much money O'Harro and Desmond spent on baseball cards and tickets: $15,000 worth, encased in resin under the bar. Patrons had reactions that ranged from not noticing to profound nostalgia. One reported, "We can look back at local sports history and remember those days. It's a real special feeling for me."[15] O.J. Simpson, during a visit in 1984, expressed surprise at finding his Bills uniform on display.[16] A later reviewer of a Champions (Marriot Hotels bought the Champions in 1992 and franchised it) asserted that "walking into a Champions feels a little like regressing to childhood and being one-upped by the kid with the biggest baseball card collection."[17]

Champions' success was unquestionable. It was "the largest grossing liquor bar per square foot in the country" and made *Playboy*'s top singles bars list in 1984. In 1986 Marriott offered to franchise the bar.[18] In 1989 Marriott, at O'Harra's direction, paid $110,000 for a painting of Mickey Mantle commissioned for the Topps Company and later used for a 1953 baseball card, part of the only series that used paintings instead of photographs. In that same year, O'Harro toured Marriot hotels in nine cities with a traveling exhibition of objects from the Topps auction.[19] In 1992, Desmond and O'Harro sold their interest in Champions to Marriott, which went on to open thirty-four locations, some overseas.[20] Marriott was not the only entity imitating the combination of sports on satellite TV (which increased the volume and variety of sports programming), historic artifacts, and mixed-sex clientele. Soon this version of the sports bar proliferated across the country, and whether they chose the singles bar model or not, bar owners used television and artifacts as the primary signifiers of the sports bar. Theming with artifacts had been a practice of American restaurants since the 1930s,[21] but the consistency and scope of using artifacts to denote "sports bar" eclipsed all other types of vernacular exhibition to date. By 1998, writer John Galvin, forgetting the deep roots of sport in the British pub tradition, pronounced the sports bar an American cultural export, with versions popping up in Japan, Mexico, Jamaica, England, and Cameroon.[22] Despite Galvin's memory lapse, his assessment was accurate in providing portrayals of the global economic practice of segmenting the entertainment sector, primarily for younger, wealthier patrons. As Robert Hollands and Paul Chatterton point out, the sports bar came of age at the beginning of "the new entertainment economy . . . distinguishable by an emerging mode of production including a concentration of corporate ownership, increased use of branding and theming, and conscious attempts to segment its markets, especially through gentrification and sanitization of leisure activities."[23]

While large bars and restaurants using themed artifact displays emphasize the popularity and profitability of theming, displays created in smaller businesses reveal more about the role of private history in public display. It is in these settings that a visitor can learn about connections between individuals and their communities.

VERNACULAR EXHIBITION CHARACTERISTICS

The most common type of display places the location—usually a restaurant or bar—in the context of family or community history. These displays assert local pride in the achievements and/or heritage of the family or community. Emil's, an Italian restaurant in Lansing, Michigan, contains a display on the history of the restaurant and its role in Lansing's more prosperous industrial past. Like larger museum exhibits, it asserts a dominant theme (albeit much more implicitly), which could be summed up as such: Emil's is a restaurant proud of both its Italian and Michigan heritages; the people of this community have liked and appreciated us since 1921, and we are aware of our significance in the history of this community. Emil's is typical of restaurant displays in that it features personal history of the original owner. Emil is everywhere present in the exhibit's photos: chatting with employees, dining with family, standing in front of his store with a dead white-tail deer brought back from a day's hunting. Emil's favorite frying pan is on display with the label: "Emil's First Grill, 1925–1961, proves his business panned out." Unlike professionalized exhibits, there are few labels. The main interpretation is either visual or delivered textually on the front of the menu. It asserts the role of history in the long life of the restaurant: "Welcome to Emil's—a restaurant with a feeling for people and history since 1921." The interpretation assumes the visitors' familiarity with the history, as in the description of Emil's commitment to community: "As many people will remember, Emil was a man who loved to help other people. . . . He was a great supporter of Father Gabriel's and Resurrection Church."[24]

Museum bars focused on sports are very much tied to place and specific fan communities. Such is the case with Famer's. The Upper Peninsula Sports Hall of Fame in Famer's Bar in Iron Mountain, Michigan, is one example of this type of approach. Located at the bottom of Pine Mountain, a ski resort specializing in ski jump competitions, the U.P. Sports Hall of Fame asserts that U.P. residents have a long history of achievement in a variety of sports. The display demonstrates that individuals from all over the U.P. have distinguished themselves in high school, amateur, and professional athletics. Composed of over a hundred and fifty objects, the display uses primarily small labels for individual objects instead of large text with broad interpretive themes, consistent with Hall of Fame practices. The interpretation focuses on location and achievement, assuming a level of familiarity

Figure 5.2. Artifacts in bars are often displayed higher and are well cased to prevent theft and damage from food and drink. (Upper Peninsula Sports Hall of Fame in Famer's Bar, Iron Mountain, Michigan. Photo by author.)

with both sports and the Upper Peninsula. A label for the ski-jumping wear display (pants, sweater, hat, goggles, and photo) illustrates the interpretive style, with the name of the Hall of Famer followed by the year of induction and object interpretation: "Don M. Hurst, Marquette (1988). Ski clothing worn by Hurst during the height of ski-jumping career including 1973 National Ski Jumping Championships at Suicide Hill in Ishpeming. Sweater hand knit by wife Georgiana."[25] References to such regional features as Suicide Hill and details such as the hand-knitting reinforce the assertion of local pride and assume the reader has some (or should have some) familiarity with the area and topic.

While some vernacular exhibitions function to authenticate place, others approach this with significant irony. The Euclid Avenue Yacht Club in the Little Five Points neighborhood of Atlanta, Georgia, is a case in point. A nautical-theme bar in landlocked Atlanta is ironic, but the play on class is also what makes this display what a bumper sticker above the dart board declares: "It's not just a bar. It's an adventure." The bar's clientele is more biker and less yachter. A Citysearch Editorial profile noted "All crowds—hippie to Harley, preppie to punk—drop anchor at the Yacht Club. The natural place to grab a beer in Little Five, this friendly joint charms with one of Atlanta's most easy-going vibes." Fishing photos, captain portraits, deep sea fish mounts, and even photos of Mikhail Barishnikov fishing and enjoying a cigar make up what the reviewer called "a packrat's closet."[26] Although started by the owners, the collection has grown through patron contributions. Staff have also added to the collection: a cook painted a portrait of Captain Smith of Titanic fame, displayed above a label that reads "We're taking on water but there's no need to panic. Capt. Edward J. Smith, the Titanic." The women's restroom has a display about early twentieth-century ads and cartoons featuring women, including an ad for a sex advice manual, a calendar, a promotional flyer encouraging a "free nationwide system of public toilets," and a framed National Women's Suffrage Association sign dated 1919, demanding Americans "Let Women Vote." Patrons enjoy the carnivalesque atmosphere created by the whole collection; one even opened a panel in the wall to show some artwork left from when the building was "some sort of artist hangout." Other patrons agreed with his interpretation of the bar, that "There are stories in these walls."[27]

Other vernacular exhibitions focus on an object collection rather than the broad themes evoked by objects that contextualize (or carnivalize) place. The Travelers Club International Restaurant and Tuba Museum in Okemos, Michigan, illustrates this type. The restaurant has dual themes of world travel and tubas, displaying textiles and masks in conjunction with a wide variety of tuba types. Like Emil's, the Travelers Club and Tuba Museum has few object labels, and delivers interpretation in the menu. Including a history of the building and the personal histories of the owners, the menu

Figure 5.3.　Display of historic ads and graphics in women's bathroom at the Euclid Avenue Yacht Club. (Little Five Points, Atlanta, Georgia, 2006. Photo by author.)

interpretation saves its most technical interpretation for tubas, instructing visitors on the instrument's history and various types. While its specificity is typical of museum exhibits' rhetoric, its tone is something different. It even explicitly makes fun of scholarly jargon: "While the common definition of the Tuba is simply a large bass horn, a scholar could correctly call it a lip-vibrated cup mouthpiece multivalved conical bored aerophone of the lower register!" Together, the international art collection and the tubas speak to the personal histories of the owners, citing travels in the 1950s and 60s and experience as a street musician in a college town in the 1960s. The emphasis on homegrown and unprocessed food in this context gives the restaurant-museum an atmosphere of 1960s bohemian reminiscence.[28]

Restaurant and bar displays obviously warrant a discussion of preservation. Preservation practices vary widely in vernacular exhibitions. For some in which access is the key to their appeal, artifacts may be easily stolen or damaged. The Pappases, owners of B&J's American Café in LaPorte, Indiana, house boxes of mid-twentieth-century photographs in a back dining room. Held in cardboard boxes that originally held food products, the photos may be perused by anyone who asks. Obviously, this open invitation appeals to patrons, and the Pappases have as yet known no photos to have been damaged or stolen. Their proximity to food and drink make damage likely, but to the owners access is a higher priority, not to mention much more feasible than a separate collections room. In bars, artifacts are usually displayed much higher than those in other vernacular exhibitions and are cased in varying ways. James Murphy, Jr., current owner of Murphy's Bleachers in Chicago, notes that his bar has always made sure the historic uniforms have solid, museum-grade plexiglass casing, and are hung well above the centerline used by museum exhibitionists. This is a preservation measure designed to prevent overexcited, intoxicated (or both) Cubs fans from taking or damaging them. In other bars artifacts hang without cases, the emphasis being on display effect and not preservation. Restaurants are more prone to fire than other types of buildings, and this has resulted in loss of artifacts. The Windy Hollow Restaurant and Museum in Owensboro, Kentucky, burned to the ground in December 2006, completely destroying all of its artifacts with the exception of a 1913 Model T, which was severely damaged.[29] Iron worker J.C. Stillwell founded The Mackinac Bridge Museum to document the construction of the Mackinac Bridge connecting Michigan's peninsulas. Housed in Mama Mia's Pizza in Mackinaw City, it burned in August 2005, taking with it a large collection of Mackinac Bridge artifacts, which included a diving suit and other belongings from ironworkers who built the bridge.[30] Sometimes vernacular exhibition helps preserve artifacts. The local historical society in Ripley, West Virginia, displays collections of primary and secondary source materials on local history, campaign buttons, and the "First Flag used by American Legion Post 107 of Ripley,

West Virginia" in cabinets in the lobby of the Best Western McCoy's Inn and Conference Center. The reason the artifacts are in the hotel lobby is that the historical society building burned and the community used the Best Western as a temporary exhibition space.

While bars and restaurants may be the most common setting for vernacular exhibitions, they are certainly not the only; barbershops are another common location. The exhibits in barbershops are usually the work of a single individual, who, while cutting hair, discusses the collection. The personality of the barber, reflected in the collection, appeals to customers. Customers also contribute to the collection, as they have to Isamu Takeda's matchbook collection in The Lanai Barber Shop in Sacramento, California: "Back when I was smoking heavy, I was always looking for matches. Whenever I went to a bar or restaurant, I would grab some. Soon I had a jar full of them. This is 42 years of collecting. It's become a community project. Customers would clean out their drawers and bring them to me. Now it's hard to find matches."[31] A customer at Tony Polito's Barber Shop and Military Museum noted "You don't come here for the haircuts, you come here for the wealth of knowledge . . . . There's no world crisis that hasn't been solved in Anthony J. Polito's Barber Shop and Military Museum." The barbershop is filled with militaria, including a swastika-adorned flag signed by the unit who brought it home from Germany after World War II.[32] While Polito's is a masculine environment, not all barbershop museums are. The three New York locations of The Barber Pole emphasize family haircuts in their re-created 1890s barbershops. Patrons can see barber poles, barbering tools, shaving mugs, and straight razors.[33]

Like some stand-alone museums, vernacular exhibits can draw heavily from nineteenth-century dime museum techniques, displaying the bizarre, the exotic, or the risqué. Ye Olde Curiosity Shop in Seattle, Washington, is where, according to its promotional/interpretive brochure, "Every single nook and cranny is brimming with astonishing, wondrous new discoveries." Part souvenir store, part dime museum, the Curiosity Shop has been at its same location since 1899. Visitors can shop for souvenir t-shirts, mugs, and joke books while they examine a diversity of artifacts. These include a World War II kamikaze flag, a two-headed calf, "Petri-fido" (a dried dog carcass), a 1920s coin-operated machine that shows a nude woman at the edge of a bathtub draped in a towel and talking on the phone, hundred-year-old fleas in dresses, a whale penis, Native American arts, and its signature object—"Sylvester," a desiccated corpse billed as "one tough cowboy." His label reads:

Meet Sylvester
"One Tough Cowboy." Featured nationally on *National Geographic*'s TV show *The Mummy Road Show*, Sylvester was coated with arsenic and as a result

he is one of the most well preserved mummies in North America. Sylvester weighs over 130 pounds and is in possession of all his internal organs, which are only about two-thirds of their original size. Get up close and personal with this "Desert Mummy" from the wild, wild west. Inspect the fatal gunshot wound to his stomach where the bullet that caused his demise revealed by X-ray and MRI. No one knows Sylvester's real story, not even his true name. Maybe you can solve the mystery of how a 45 year old man wound up nude and half-buried in the sands of the Gila Bend Desert.[34]

Cashiers are quick to leave the till and add further details for this compelling corpse. According to one cashier, Sylvester used to be displayed in a coffin, but visitors kept touching him. The arsenic was not good for the visitors and the touching was not good for Sylvester, and so the owners changed his display to a vertical Plexiglas case, with a miniature gift shop "Indian Blanket" covering his genitalia.

Some of the best examples of vernacular exhibitions can be found in thrift stores, whose popularity (not to mention sheer square footage) seems to have grown in conjunction with the decrease in industrial sector jobs in rustbelt areas. These stores provide a first draft of material culture history, a space in which value is reclaimed and objects are saved from destruction. In such a setting, thrift store staff rises to the occasion, by creating historical interpretations to help stock move. They often employ fairly loose standards of accuracy, but nevertheless interpret history. One interesting example is from Valueland in Lansing, Michigan, a thrift store supporting Christian missionary work. Its 1970s display combines a couple of signifiers to evoke that period. Polyester shirts and bell-bottoms, whether from the 1970s or the more recent retro trend, are collected for this rack and topped with a pink shirt over a red turtleneck next to a box hand painted and decorated "70's." Stuck atop the box is the obligatory bicentennial referent, the small American flag. The objects used to tell this history are cast off; their values are in limbo. The thrift store staff asserted that these particular objects were valuable because they help us to remember and reconstruct the past.[35]

While the seventies display in Valueland is obviously for sale (although I would not want to be the shopper who ruined the effect), other vernacular exhibitions can confuse the artifact/commodity distinction. Located in the Blue Island area of Chicago since 1894, Jebens Hardware Store is the area's most long-lasting business. Owner Art Bulmann said Jebens was "the Ed Debevic's of hardware stores," referring to the Chicago hamburger joint famous for evoking nostalgia. Writer Scott Broden noted that the dominance of artifacts, which include gas pumps, soda machines, and multiple cigar store Indians, "challeng(es) shoppers to detect which items are for sale and which are for show."[36] So mingled are the commodity and show items, visiting the display is an exercise in distinguishing not only past from present but each object's status vis-à-vis the consumer.

Figure 5.4. Sylvester, signature mummy at Ye Olde Curiosity Shop. "Petri-Fido," a dessicated dog carcass, hangs above him. The shop represents a tradition of dime museum display, emphasizing the exotic. (Ye Olde Curiosity Shop, Seattle, Washington, 2005. Photo by author.)

Figure 5.5. A thrift store worker's take on the 1970s. (ValueLand World Mission Thrift, Lansing, Michigan, 2004. Photo by author.)

Some displays can change meaning over time from one topic to another. This is the case with Mary and Moe's Wigwam in Fernley, Nevada. When Mary and Moe Royels sold The Wigwam to Holder Hospitality Group in 2005, the restaurant housed around five hundred artifacts relating to Native Americans. Instead of being used to interpret Native American life, the artifacts came to symbolize the lives of the Royels. Moe Royels grew up on the Wadsworth reservation, his father a principal of the local school. Collecting artifacts reminded him of growing up. When the Royels married in 1964, they changed the name of Mary's restaurant from The Dainty Cone to Mary and Moe's Wigwam. Over forty-one years of business, it came to evoke its collectors, not its subject. The community regarded the Royels highly, and both were active in the community. The restaurant "really was the town center," noted resident Willie Shay. Mary Royels reported that men met in the dining room before six in the morning to talk and "solve the world's problems." The Holder Hospitality Group hoped the Royels would be "ambassadors" for the new management, a role they were happy to fill: "This is the only thing we've ever done in our whole lives . . . . We wouldn't know how to live anywhere else." When the Royels sold the restaurant, they loaned the collection to the new owners and continued to eat there regularly until Mary Royels' death in 2007.[37]

Jim Murphy left his legacy, as well as his collection, in Murphy's Bleachers, a favorite bar of Chicago Cubs fans. A "Bleachers" bar has been on the corner of Waveland and Sheffield across from Wrigley Field since the 1930s. Named after its owners, first Ernie's Bleachers and then Ray's Bleachers, the bar became Murphy's Bleachers in 1980, when Chicago police officer Jim Murphy bought it and began to display Cubs and other sports artifacts. Expanding rapidly, Murphy's Bleachers grew to include several bars, including the original bar, an Irish bar, a rooftop bar and the "South Bar."[38] The exhibits are highly photographic, documenting the changes in Wrigleyville and the history of the Cubs. Textiles are the next most common artifact type, with uniforms dating from the 1930s to the present. Some are associated with the big names of Cubs history—Sandberg, Myers, Banks—while others are generic Cubs jackets and uniforms. Murphy's Bleachers exhibits also include items salvaged from the stadium itself, or items that speak to changes in Wrigley Field, such as the "Let There Be Lights In Wrigley Field" placard. In this way, the artifacts document not only the history of a baseball team but the history of its fans as well. Because the artifacts were collected by one man, the late Jim Murphy, a former police officer, neighborhood activist, and devoted fan, the collection also documents a more personal history.

Jim Murphy most clearly exemplified the vernacular exhibition curator's role as community activist. His collecting was the quietest of his community-focused activities (besides anonymous philanthropy). When Murphy

Figure 5.6.   Artifacts relating to the lights controversy at Wrigley Field. (Murphy's Bleachers, Chicago, Illinois, 2006. Photo by author.)

first bought his bar in 1980, he was one of the few who saw the business potential of the area surrounding Wrigley Field. Not yet the gentrified Wrigleyville, the neighborhood "had gangs with shootouts on the corner. Property values were down to rock bottom," reported Michael LaVelle, Chicago lawyer and friend of Murphy.[39] Murphy brought new ideas about marketing and fully embraced the new breed of sports bar that relied on history (and historical artifacts), a mixed-sex clientele, television, and placed-based sports theming.[40] As late as 1990, he was seen as a bit of an upstart by old-time Lake View baseball fans. When Ray Meyer, who sold the bar to Murphy in 1980 returned shortly after the sale, he noted: "I almost fell over when I saw it. They took the baseball out of it. It's almost like Rush Street,"[41] referring to the area Citysearch currently calls "the city's most happening party strip." The "party" aspect of Murphy's Bleachers was ultimately what contributed to its major success, and it paralleled changes in the neighborhood. Castas Spirou and Larry Bennett describe the Wrigleyville transition from neighborhood to entertainment complex, initially enabled by night games at Wrigley Field:

> The emergence of the new Lake View that has coincided with the advent of nighttime baseball at Wrigley Field represents a strikingly ambiguous story of neighborhood transformation. The area immediately adjacent to the ballpark has become an entertainment center whose multitude of nightclubs, restaurants, sports bars and souvenir shops attract customers throughout the year. While it is obvious that the modernizing of Wrigley Field contributed to the emergence of this wildly popular district, with each passing year it becomes equally evident that the allure of "Wrigleyville," a designation generally despised by local residents, transcends the allure of baseball.[42]

As the night games brought increased business to Murphy's Bleachers, Jim Murphy expanded the bar in size and in its artifact holdings, collecting not just Cubs memorabilia, but sporting and neighborhood artifacts from throughout Chicago. Even while he was a significant force in Wrigleyville's transformation, he kept emphasizing its historic qualities. By 1995, Murphy's Bleachers was something of a historic institution, attesting not to the changes but to the stability of the neighborhood, and retired Cubs pitcher Rick Sutcliffe named Jim Murphy in a list of things that had not changed since his pitching days in the 80s. Before Murphy became embroiled in a dispute with the Cubs over bleacher expansion, he was quoted in the *Sun-Times* as being concerned over maintaining the tradition of rooftop parties. When in 1998 the city indicated the rooftop parties needed to be regulated for safety, Jim Murphy immediately started investing in "fire safety improvements in anticipation of the ordinance," to keep the tradition alive. Murphy recalled the low-key parties of the past as the ancestor of the late-nineties business version.[43] His rooftop business had grown enough for him to invest significantly in it, dropping between $400,000 and $500,000 to comply with the ordinance. The signal that the rooftop business had really arrived was the addition of an artifact: a piece of Comiskey Park scoreboard. Its installation led Murphy to explain that civic pride crosses teams: "We're Chicago sports fans, not just Cubs . . . . If we went to a White Sox game, we'd be rooting for them, too."[44]

Jim Murphy's civic allegiances would soon be questioned publicly, in a debate brought on by the 2001 plan for bleacher expansion unveiled by the Cubs. A review of news coverage of his involvement with the bleacher controversy, however, reveals him to be just as interested in community issues as in his own business interests. Before the Cubs revealed bleacher expansion plans, Murphy expressed publicly that they might interfere with rooftop views. When the plans became public, they included not just bleacher expansion but plans for more night games. Murphy commented on both, saying that day games were better for his business and that the plans would interfere with his rooftop business. He also worried for the historic integrity of the stadium itself, a concern he would repeat later in the controversy in reference to the proposed idea that rooftop businesses simply increase building height: "We're trying to preserve the historic look of the area here, and that just doesn't do it. It can't look like they're building an aircraft carrier out there," Murphy said of the rise in height restrictions and one rooftop's initial effort at rising to them.[45] By early 2002 the feud was getting ugly, and Murphy, as president of the Wrigleyville Rooftop Owners Association and chair of the East Lake View Neighbors, drew increased public attention, with the Cubs vice president of business operations Mark McGuire accusing him of "conflict of interest" and *Sun-Times* readers accusing him of catering to elite fans and stealing the "Cubs product."[46] Murphy continued to comment not just on the rooftop business but on neighborhood quality-of-life problems like public urination, safe sidewalks, and fair compensation to the city for the Cubs' use of property.[47] When neighborhood groups successfully changed Mayor Daley's mind about the expansion and he blocked its progress, the Cubs responded by installing netting in the stadium, blocking views from the outside. They cited security concerns stemming from post-9/11 surveys of the facility but later acknowledged the desire to "play hardball" with the rooftop owners, who had hired their own PR firm.[48] When Daley issued the final verdict on expansion—"no additional night games in 2003, no sidewalk pillars to support more bleachers, and fair-market rent for property the team has had for free"[49]—and Planning Commissioner Alicia Berg lifted the freeze on giving the field landmark status,[50] the Cubs filed a copyright suit against owners of thirteen rooftop businesses. Murphy's take on their actions emphasized that the neighborhood is part of what has made Wrigley Field so successful:

> They can't attack the community, so they chose us, but they're going to embarrass themselves in the long run . . . . People have been charged for being on roof decks since the first day Wrigley opened in 1914. The Cubs allowed the city to license us without objection. They have given the tacit OK to the fact that roof decks exist. I can't understand why the Cubs want to change a historical ballpark and make it more like Comiskey by taking the roof decks away.

They don't understand that the neighborhood is what made Wrigley Field what it is. It's not the team's playing ability.[51]

When Jim Murphy was next mentioned in a Chicago newspaper, it would be in his obituary. The fifty-four-year-old died of cancer on January 28, 2003, leaving the Wrigleyville community without its most visible spokesperson. The *Chicago Tribune* (owned by the Tribune Company, owners of the Cubs) memorialized him by saying "It was only natural that with Mr. Murphy's personality and long involvement with community organizations that he would be a central figure in the rooftop club owners' dispute with the Cubs over an expansion that would add about 2,000 seats in Wrigley." The *Sun-Times* stressed his role in community renewal.[52] Since Jim Murphy's death, the rooftop owners settled with the Cubs, and the Cubs went ahead with a bleacher expansion that accommodated concerns of neighborhood associations. Murphy's Bleachers, run by Murphy's son James, continues to be a top-rated sports bar and highly successful community fixture. The collections remain a vernacular exhibition informed by the intersection of history, individual personality, business, and community.

VISITORS AND THE MEANING OF DISPLAYED HISTORY

It is clear that curator/business owners mediate the visitor experience of the past, but visitors bring ideas of their own, and many of these ideas depend upon the past as a way of providing community connectedness in the present. They view artifacts in terms of their own identities and make consumer choices based on that identification with the history presented, a significant difference between accessing the past in the vernacular exhibition and accessing it in an academically driven exhibition in a professionalized museum. To fully explore this dynamic, we need to follow Kurt Dewhurst and Marsha MacDowell's suggestion for understanding the museum bar: place it in its community context.[53] Murphy's Bleachers demonstrates that artifacts in the sports bar stand as evidence of the strength and longevity of a community organized by its habits, in this case allegiance to the Cubs and to drinking.

The following discussion is based on results from twenty-five face-to-face interviews conducted with patrons at Murphy's Bleachers on June 27 and 28 between 11:00 a.m. and 5:00 p.m., both times preceding games at Wrigley Field. Respondents were part of visitor groups totaling sixty-seven people. The average number of people per visitor group was 2.68. The first part of the survey, consisting of eight questions about visitor opinions and museum-going habits, was conducted orally while the surveyor recorded visitor responses. While the questions were asked of individuals, sometimes other visitors contributed to the individuals' responses. The survey included seven open-ended questions and one structured response question. The second part, consisting of questions on demographic characteristics, was conducted with survey cards filled out by visitors. These cards contained only structured response questions.

In some respects, bar patrons and museum visitors were the same. Demographically, Murphy's Bleachers patrons were rather comparable to museum visitors at the National Museum of American History, with the exception of sex; respondents at Murphy's were overwhelmingly male (N=18). Nearly one-third of the sample reported being between twenty-one and thirty, which was slightly less than NMAH's 36 percent attendance by visitors between nineteen and thirty-four. Race and formal education level were typical of NMAH museum visitors.[54] A little over one-third reported visiting one or fewer history museums in the past year, but 44 percent reported having made between two and six visits to history museums in the past year. The sample had a high education level—indicating they had experience with more formal environments for learning history—and they expressed a fairly high interest in learning about the past. Overall, they were "typical" history museum visitors (with the exception of the dominance of males in the sample). The major difference between Murphy's patrons and NMAH visitors was that bar patrons separated learning history from tradition: tradition meant participation in an event, not an outsider's analysis of it.

Three-fifths of the sample said they came to Murphy's either because of tradition or because it was an assumed part of seeing a Cubs game. The word "tradition" came up consistently in the interviews, with patrons mentioning it as the reason for visiting, as the main theme of the exhibit, and as a method of hearing about the bar. Their relationship to the past had a fairly presentist focus; that is, they felt connected to the past when they came to Murphy's but they did not talk about specific events or people of the past. Only one respondent mentioned a specific individual and historic event: he had come in looking to see the Ryne Sandberg jersey and related specific details of Sandberg's first games with the Cubs. He said the jersey "reminds him of years of watching [the Cubs], sometimes agonizingly watching them."[55] Several visitors reported not knowing when they first heard about the bar, insisting they had "always known" about Murphy's. Others felt the message of the exhibits was about the long tradition of team loyalty in Wrigleyville, and had either brought friends to see the displays or had been brought by someone to see them. This emphasis on tradition is where Murphy's patrons differ from visitors to NMAH. While there is an oral tradition element to NMAH visitation (fourteen percent of visitors reported the reason for visiting was that they heard about it from friends or family), the most cited reason was an existing interest in American history: 61 percent of the sample identified this as the reason for coming to the museum.[56]

Like museum visitors in general, patrons reflected different levels of engagement in the history of baseball. One visitor group—four retirees from Canada traveling together—had made baseball museums featured destinations in their travels, and saw their visit to Murphy's as a pilgrimage of sorts. They had been to the Negro Leagues Baseball Museum, the Little League World Series Museum, and the National Baseball Hall of Fame and Museum in Cooperstown, New York. Owner James Murphy noted that wait staff does not approach visitors to the main bar immediately to allow them time to look at the artifacts.[57] Others were decidedly not there to think about the Cubs or Wrigleyville or perhaps even baseball. One reported he looked at the displays "for as long as it takes to drink a beer." Even one of the seasoned baseball museum visitors ranked beer first, heritage second, reporting that he was "too thirsty to look" at the displays but planned to once the beer had been served.[58]

Another level of engagement had to do with suburbanites' perceptions of the city and nostalgia for their version of the city. They saw Murphy's as representative of Chicago; coming to a Cubs game and visiting Murphy's gave them an authentic "city" experience. One visitor, a companion to an interview subject, candidly noted "I don't know much about Murphy's. I want to come down here more but I'm scared." Wrigleyville has recently been part of the urban gentrification movement, and the Cubs franchise has been a significant factor in that. Respondents regularly noted that the exhibits featured the history of the neighborhood, even though all artifacts and photos are about changes in the team, the stadium, or the fans coming from or going to games; there is no interpretation of suburbanization and white flight and the more recent gentrification. One respondent explained that the "neighborhood" means Cubs fans, not the people who actually live there; he said the exhibit "conveys the neighborhood, that it's centered around the ball field for generations of fans."[59] The neighborhood tavern, in its transformation to large, mixed-sex clientele sports bar, became representative of a community that does not reside nearby.[60] It is a chance for suburbanites to claim an urban heritage, and in the process of gentrification, reclaim a space almost abandoned by the white middle class in an earlier era. This dynamic represents the pilgrimage aspect of the reliquary theming identified by Alan Beardsworth and Alan Bryman[61] as well as the function of artifacts in producing fan and community legitimacy.

The curators and visitors of vernacular exhibits do not separate history from business, or producer/consumer and community identities, as more professionalized museum and museum visitors attempt to do. History and business go hand in hand because patrons—through their consumption—connect with historical ideas associated with the topic and the business that displays the topic. Moreover, they connect with the vernacular curator as a leader in the community. The ideas presented by the artifacts build community cohesion, and patrons see the business' interests to be in line with the interests of the community. While not at all exclusively responsible for community building, the exhibits function to create an atmosphere in which patrons feel a sense of belonging to something larger than their identities as consumers.

6

Local History, Global Economy: The Functions of History Exhibits in the Settings of Everyday Life

Community, entrepreneurial, and vernacular history exhibits (and the combinations of these types) have become ubiquitous on the American landscape over the last sixty years, the result of several important changes in United States economy, society, and culture. Economic globalization and the increased presence of highly produced mass media have created a demand for local "flavor": local history is one backlash against the perception that globalization has homogenized culture and a backlash against the perception that culture is produced by big companies elsewhere. These trends coincided with heightened public dialogue on identity politics, which has encouraged historical inquiry at the community and familial levels.

The increase in historical exhibition in the spaces of everyday life, while heavily informed by market forces, has led to increased opportunity for informal intergroup and individualized dialogue on historical (and hence contemporary) topics. With global commerce and communication as foils for the "authentic" experience, history exhibits in the settings of everyday life have encouraged people to share their private and individualized histories with one another. My contention is that while the history presented at these exhibits does not always measure up to academic standards of objectivity and analysis (as explained in the first chapter), and while these exhibits can be highly informed by consumerism, they can and do play a profound role in American life. Unlike most visitors to academic or corporate exhibits, visitors to community, entrepreneurial, and vernacular exhibits are likely to come face-to-face with the people who created the exhibit, those who have a personal connection to the topic. While not all these exhibits live up to their potential as facilitators of intergroup dialogue (or even as sources of accurate information), many do, and their contribution is significant enough to warrant attention from scholars and support from the broader museum community and the public at large. In order to fully understand the roles played by community, entrepreneurial, and vernacular exhibitions, we need to first examine the factors that led to their growth.

THE HISTORICAL ROOTS OF HISTORY
EXHIBITS IN THE SPACES OF DAILY LIFE

While the practice of local and familial history exhibition dates much earlier, the contemporary phenomena of historical display in businesses and promotion of local history museums for tourist trade has its roots in the 1950s and 60s. The Cold War reinforced the idea that democratic citizenship and mass consumption depended on one another; the highway system increased domestic tourism; Disney became the much-imitated model for themed environments; and markets increasingly became segmented, leading shoppers to believe that their material goods represented their identities. These phenomena—some more subtly than others—laid the groundwork for the ubiquity of historical display.

The idea that learning history is an important duty for patriotic citizens had emerged in United States history instruction in the nineteenth century, but during the Cold War it gained urgency. In the wake of social unrest it took new form. While history instruction with the purpose of creating a better citizenry did not go away in the 1960s, it was transformed to include ethnic history, urban history, and women's history.[1] The National Historic Preservation Act of 1966 was partially motivated by the sense that American things testified to the strength of America itself. It provided tax breaks, loans, and grants to support the preservation of landmarks of historical significance. These landmarks would in turn remind Americans of their democratic legacy and inspire them to become better, more patriotic citizens. This idea peaked around the time of the American bicentennial, and was reworked as marginalized groups demonstrated how the American democratic experiment benefited some over others. Tilden Rhea has shown that historic sites provided the focal point for marginalized groups to express what he called "race pride," a movement in the 1970s and 80s away from a focus on civil rights and toward respect for ethnic identity. He chronicled interpretive changes at Little Bighorn National Battlefield, the Martin Luther King, Jr., Birthplace, and the Alamo, and the emergence of Manzanar as a national historic park. Ethnic groups brought about these changes and at the same time promoted pride in and organization around ethnic identity.[2] These changes at the national level built upon the idea that learning and preserving the past created better citizens; one's duty as a citizen now included the exploration of the history of groups traditionally marginalized from the benefits of democratic capitalism.

A similar change took place in material culture, as ideas about material goods moved from American consensus to more individualized American identity. The idea that national identity should be expressed in consumables had its roots in the early twentieth century, when market segmentation had not fully come into its post-1960 popularity. Marketers promoted the idea that access to a full range of consumer goods was as American as voting. During World War II, advertisers asserted that "the boys" were fighting for American prosperity as well as freedom. Postwar access to car tires and electric mixers, in the logic of marketers, motivated men to fight. One remarkable 1944 ad for Westinghouse Electric Home Appliances used a museum trope to demonstrate the "still finer things to come" the way of consumers at the war's conclusion. A young couple stands behind a velvet stantion in front of an art museum display of paintings. Household appliances large and small appear in the paintings, each one individually portrayed and carefully framed. A sink, a stove, an iron, a vacuum cleaner, a fan, and other products overwhelm the wife, whose sense of wonder is indicated by the open expression of her arms. The husband leans forward past the velvet ropes, inspecting the details. The tag line reads: "The Art of Better Living: Yesterday . . . Today . . . Tomorrow . . . it's Electrical Living by Westinghouse."[3] This ad reveals more than wartime yearning. It foretells the expansion of museum display to a day when manufactured, even common, goods become worthy of exhibition. It would take further analysis of the national narrative, but eventually everyone's goods would become the stuff of exhibits.

Starting in the 1950s, market segmentation became increasingly common and by the 1970s it connected to the "race pride" movement in ways that validated the idea that one's things stood for one's identity. As Lizabeth Cohen has shown, market segmentation started as an advertising technique that conceived of the public not as a mass but as an almost infinitely divisible populace, with each division receiving its own advertising approach. The passage of the Immigration and Nationality Act of 1965 led to the increase of non-European immigration and further diversified the American populace. By the 1970s market segmentation would be validated by not only this increased diversification of society but by the cultural and political movements surrounding various markers of identity: race, sex, sexual orientation, class, age, ethnicity.[4] These movements rightly questioned the "grand narrative" of American history and promoted inquiry into the history of marginalized groups; this inquiry could be expressed through shopping and displaying the goods representing one's family, community, and identity.

By the late 1970s and early 80s, Americans had combined their shopping and their politics and increasingly used material culture to assert identity.[5] The transformation and survival of the notion that it is one's duty as a citizen to learn the country's history fed the national interest in exploring the cultures that made up the country's population, and academic and popular

Figure 6.1 . Consumer goods and the museum trope. Advertisement from *Life*, September 25, 1944. (Courtesy of Westinghouse Electric Corporation.)

history alike focused on previously ignored groups. Marketers and makers of consumer goods—already heavily invested in market segmentation—responded to this interest with advertising and products aimed at particular demographics like young African American males, white women in their forties, descendents of Scottish immigrants, gay men.[6] The tourism industry also responded with "homeland" tours.[7] The idea that learning history was one's civic duty merged with the notion that one's identity should be represented through consumption and supported the logic that consumer spaces, as well as other public spaces, should include material evidence of local, community, or family heritage. Displaying one's identity for others became part of living one's identity.

By the 1980s, market segmentation fueled increased fetishization of goods, and consumerism grew even as many Americans struggled with strained incomes and shortened leisure time. Juliet Schor best articulated the related phenomena of the decrease in leisure time and rampant consumerism in the post-1980 period with her two works *The Overworked American: The Unexpected Decline of Leisure* (1991) and *The Overspent American: Upscaling, Downshifting, and the New Consumer* (1998). Schor described a shift in American society in which people found themselves working longer and longer to make up for an "aspirational gap" between the lifestyles of the wealthy few and nonwealthy many. Starting around 1980, those with incomes in the upper 20 percent began to increase in wealth and at the same time set consumer habits for those in the lower 80 percent who were losing wealth. The notion that "we are what we own" took a stranglehold on Americans, and found expression through clothes, cars, homes, and electronics. One result has been increased consumption paired with increased debt.[8] Another result has been the increased fetishization of material culture, whether first- or secondhand goods.

The collector market followed the general upswing in consumerism, and no phenomenon represents this trend better than eBay. Ken Hillis, Michael Petit, and Nathan Scott Epley provide solid evidence of the online auction house's success, which began in 1996:

> During the second quarter of 2005 alone, eBay had over 440 million listings and 157.3 million registered users worldwide . . . . In 2004, the website facilitated international gross sales of more than 34 billion USD in merchandise, and in 2005 was on target to facilitate over 40 billion. Each day, sellers list 4.89 million items organized across more than 40,000 main and subcategories that continually expand in number. Five hundred thousand Americans, eBay estimates, make all or part of their living from selling on its site in 2005.[9]

eBay had tapped into an already lively collector culture in the United States. *The Antiques Roadshow* was the most popular show on PBS. Baseball memorabilia, lunch boxes, and beanie babies had fetched absurdly high prices.

By 2001, *Kovel's Antiques and Collectibles* listed $25 for a 1995 Cincinnati Reds Wheaties box, $770 for a 1912 Coca-Cola glass, $3,300 for a Heddon Black Sucker Minnow fishing lure, and $5,200 for a Bowman 1951 Mickey Mantle baseball card, No. 253.[10] Russell Belk interviewed collectors in the early nineties, and found that for collectors, collecting meant "gaining a feeling of mastery, competence, or success . . . . In a materialistic society, the quality and quantity of our possessions are broadly assumed to be an index of our successfulness in life in general. In addition, by competing for objects of rare value, we are able to demonstrate our relative prowess and the efforts of superior knowledge, tenacity, monetary resources, cleverness, or luck."[11] Like first-hand goods, one's possession of antiques and collectibles supposedly reflects something positive about their owners. This has led to an increased display of one's goods.

The new consumerist fetishization of goods coincided with a rise in Americans' media exposure. Media scholar Todd Gitlin summed up the recent increase in media exposure by asserting "it is clear that the media flow into the home—not to mention outside—has swelled to a torrent of immense force and constancy, an accompaniment *to* life that has become a central experience *of* life."[12] Not only did Americans' movies, television, and print media become more sophisticated in their production, by 1999 business executive and scholars alike had noted that Americans' very *experiences* had reached an unprecedented level of management and production, as themed environments like Hard Rock Café and Cabela's sought to add value to their products by giving customers a sense of being in a place apart from the ordinary.[13] The globalization of the economy, particularly the expansion of American service and retail companies to foreign markets, added to the sense that big companies controlled culture, forcing the same products on diverse peoples across the globe. This perception increased the appeal of local heritage,[14] which provided a "boutique" cultural experience, and led business owners and citizens to step up displays of their histories. Local heritage became a panacea for the globalizing and faceless companies that brought culture to mass audiences.

FUNCTIONS OF HISTORICAL DISPLAY
IN THE SETTINGS OF DAILY LIFE

The increase in the consumer economy, tourism, market segmentation, and public dialogue on identity fueled the creation and use of community, entrepreneurial, and vernacular exhibitions. These causes, however, do not explain them entirely. As any museum educator will assert, curators and visitors create meaning together. Economic and cultural forces may have inspired them, but individuals react to them in unique ways. Some visitors, usually looking in from the outside, want to get information that is not mediated by big government or big business. Other visitors feel intimately connected to a community by being surrounded by its artifacts; artifacts validate their inclusion. Still others, whether intimately connected to the history or not, simply seek opportunity for conversation about the past, and find it in community, entrepreneurial, and vernacular exhibitions. These conversations and new insights on the history of others can be the seeds of empathy, the beginning of intergroup dialogue.

From the visitor's perspective, face-to-face conversation is the most significant difference between a visit to a large history museum and a small, local history museum. In summer 2006 a visitor group of six from Denmark, consisting of two parents in their forties, two children in their teens, and two young adults, visited the Shoshone-Bannock Tribal Museum on the Fort Hall Reservation in rural Idaho. They had been driving by on the highway, saw the sign for the museum, and stopped out of curiosity. The tourists stayed in the gallery for over an hour, talking with one another about the objects and photos. When they emerged, they engaged the museum manager in conversation for an additional half hour. Most of the conversation revolved around photos of Shoshones and Bannocks taken in the nineteenth century by Danish immigrant Benedicte Wrensted. The museum manager and the adults of the visitor group consulted and discussed some of the reference books from the museum's library. The visitor group left with a list of books about Shoshone-Bannock tribal history written out for them by the museum manager.

By most measures of museum visitor experience, the visit was a success: they stayed in the gallery for much longer than most visits;[15] they conversed with each other in the gallery; they initiated conversation with a museum employee;[16] and they left with a tool for learning more. This visit demonstrates the importance of the community exhibit to international dialogue on history and culture. The small museum provides an intimacy that is lacking in larger, highly professionalized museums in the United States. This feature is more conducive to face-to-face conversation between people of differing nationalities, something sociologist John Urry calls the "globalization of intermittent co-presence," which he sees as important to a healthy society. The interactions must be profound enough to inform individuals' decisions beyond the duration of the co-presence, because the "connections derived from co-presence can generate relations of trust that enhance both social and economic inclusion."[17]

Unlike the large museums, where visitors interact primarily with technologies, small museums provide ample opportunity for meaningful co-presence. First, smaller galleries and office spaces require closer physical proximities between curators and visitors. Second, curators at small museums are more likely to take on multiple roles, providing collections care and interpretation as well as visitor services. Visitors are more likely to come face-to-face with the people who did the research. Third, many smaller museums have close spatial ties to small business functions. Many small museums connect to restaurants, bars, print shops, or plumbing supply houses (for example), and the multifunctionality of the space encourages informal conversation. Finally, the curators are more likely to have personal connections to the historical topic and draw heavily from it for identity formation, adding to the "authenticity" of the visitor experience.

These features add up to significant opportunity for meaningful conversations between people of different nationalities, cultures, ethnicities, and regions. "We look for museums just like this," noted twenty-five-year-old Norwegian Lars Gjertveit of the Lone Jack Civil War Museum, a small museum in Missouri run by self-taught historian Irene Spainhour. As the only visitors that day, the Norwegians received the curator's "undivided attention."[18] Curators, particularly in community and entrepreneurial exhibitions, specialize in conversation. "He had a good spiel and would play something to the hilt," reported the son of Gordon Hodgin, a "local storyteller [and] amateur historian" active in the Delta County (Colorado) Historical Museum. Locally known as the man who refused a Smithsonian Institution request to purchase a butterfly collection held by the museum, Hodgin's allegiance to community and museum were indistinguishable, and both were reflected in his desire to engage and entertain visitors; his willingness to represent the community through its museum and his "flair . . . made history come alive" for his audience.[19] Lynne Iorio summed up many volunteers' motivations for working at historical society museums: "I wanted to do something that was with people . . . so I volunteered for the [museum]."[20] Howard Wetlians, curator of the African-American Sports Museum in Cobb County, Georgia, emphasized visitor communication: "To say I have a museum is fun . . . but I want to touch people."[21] This attention to visitor engagement at small museums meets with frequent success. One volunteer at a local history museum in North Carolina noted that "people come in and, when they get ready to leave, they don't realize how long they've been in here."[22] One visitor to the Olde Mill House Printing Museum simply noted the museum was "a nice place to have a conversation."[23] The small museum—with its decentralized authority, its hybrid epistemology, its intimate spaces, its local curators, and its interesting objects—breaks down traditional museum hierarchies to function as an ideal site for informal public conversation among strangers. The small museum effectively complicates the traditional (and often uncomfortable) dichotomies between curator/visitor, subject/object, and public/private.

While conversation is one visitor motivator, a search for "the real" is another. Scholar Amy Levin notes that nontraditional museums "occupy a particular niche in our evolving social grammar, one that reflects not only cultural change, but also reactionary forces and attempts at subversion."[24] Small museums are stunningly diverse in topic and approach. At a gift shop in Seattle, visitors can see the desiccated remains of a nineteenth-century cowboy or operate an early twentieth-century risqué photo machine. At countless local historical societies, visitors can understand the development of small communities from the point of view of their citizens. They can learn about small industry or obsolete skills from the people who still practice them. If they visit enough small museums they can see the United States at its most diverse and quirky, but also at its most prejudiced, as studies of plantation houses and community memorials have shown.[25] The New Orleans Historic Voodoo Museum and the Avery House Museum in Fort Collins, Colorado, are representative of small museum diversity. These two are very different in terms of theme and interpretive approach. The Avery House, run by an all-volunteer staff, has an annual visitation between 4,000 and 5,000. It interprets the history of the Avery family: "Built in 1879, The Avery House represents the gains made by those 'founding fathers' of Fort Collins who committed themselves to the economic development of the town of Fort Collins."[26] It is typical of Victorian house museum interpretation in its focus on the wealth and activities of its founder: the classic American "great man" story. The Voodoo Museum is funded exclusively by admission fees and the gift shop, and had an annual visitation of 20,000 before Hurricane Katrina (in fall 2006, the museum reported an annual visitation around 4,300).[27] Its focus is significantly less genteel—promotional literature advertises visitors can learn "How to make a zombie and how to avoid one!"— but the museum is no less committed to the interpretation of a unique history. These two very different museums are alike in their drive to collect and display their past, and in configuring the past as a marker of group identity. The increase in venues of historical interpretation—what one scholar has called "the heritage crusade"[28]—is the result of a global economy perceived as having a homogenizing effect on culture, thereby making the local even more interesting, and hence marketable. Fort Collins and New Orleans have this in common with villages and cities from Iceland to Indonesia: local heritage is a commodity in the global economy.[29]

International tourists' visits to small museums reveal the potential of small museums to engage visitors across national boundaries. The United States ranks third in the world in international tourist arrivals and leads the world in international tourism receipts.[30] While international tourists seek the major attractions like theaters, national museums, and national parks, they also find their way to small history museums. In a ten-month period in 2007–2008, the Rock and Roll and Blues Heritage Museum in Clarksdale, Mississippi, received over twenty visitors from outside the United States. Hailing from England, Norway, Belgium, India, Canada, Sweden, Germany, Costa Rica, France, and the Netherlands, these visitors examined musical history artifacts such as LP covers, posters, concert tickets, and guitars, and read about Clarksdale's homegrown musical talent: John Lee Hooker, Little Junior Parker, Lil Green, Ike Turner, Sam Cooke, and Muddy Waters. All but two of the visitors stayed between thirty minutes and two hours in the 3,000 square feet of gallery space. They had heard of the museum from diverse sources: friends or relatives, travel agents, brochures or guidebooks, or from local business owners. Four had just been out looking for something to do when they happened upon the museum. All but one of them said they enjoyed the museum so much they would recommend the museum to their friends and family. They loved the collection and the histories represented there. One French visitor reported the visit "reminded us of our own youthful 'rock'."[31] Others mentioned the "nice" or "knowledgeable" owner. One was inspired to reflect on more theoretical issues:"History is knowledge. It needs to be passed on!"[32] Such engagement echoes that of museum owner and founder Theo Dasbach, who started the museum in 1995 in The Netherlands, but ten years later brought his passion to Clarksdale, home to so much of the history his museum tells. Theo Dasbach and his visitors are just one example of an important phenomenon in heritage tourism and of American life in general.

Surveys, face-to-face interviews, visitor logs, and press coverage of international visitation indicate that small museums are serving international visitors with significant opportunities for meaningful exchange across borders. A 2006 needs assessment survey of small museums in the United States yielded information that demonstrates a need for further study of international visitation at small museums.[33] Thirty-one out of forty-two respondents to the survey included information on the last fifty visitors who signed their guest book. These showed:

- Eighteen small museums (56 percent of the sample) had at least one international visitor group.
- These eighteen small museums served a total of sixty-five international visitor groups representing nineteen countries.
- The UK was the largest exporter of visitor groups (N=29), followed by Germany (N=9) and Canada (N=5).
- While most visitor groups came from Western Europe (N=46), Eastern Europe, Asia, Africa, and North America were also represented.

A survey of international visitors at nineteen small museums—diverse in topic and exhibit characteristics—between November of 2007 and September of 2008 produced seventy responses from seven museums. Some sites reported having international visitors who declined the opportunity to take a survey, while others had no international visitors at all. While the precise number of international visitors at small museums in the United States is difficult to determine, these sources indicate that small museums are serving international visitors.

International visitors to these museums reveal visitor behavior patterns that are similar to those of domestic visitors. International visitors learned of the museum from diverse sources (although they were slightly more dependent on guidebooks). They reported slightly longer visits, and they were less likely to be repeat visitors. Like domestic visitors, international visitors found significant connections to place and people at the small museum through both differences and similarities to their own countries. One Costa Rican visitor group reported they would recommend the lighthouse museum at Smith Island, North Carolina, because it was "something very different from what we'd find in our country."[34] A visitor from India at North Carolina's Fort Fisher State Historic Site, a Civil War site with earthworks, interpretive exhibits, tours, and weapons displays, likewise planned to bring home the knowledge learned at the site. He wrote: "The demonstrations and audiovisuals are very good. I wouldn't have got a feel of the battle otherwise. . . . I hail from Mumbai, India. We have as many as 350 forts in our state and each fort has its distinct battle history. I would try to get this idea back home so that we would be able to make the demos realistic like this museum."[35] One Australian couple visiting the Olde Mill House Printing Museum in Homosassa, Florida, observed that the museum was evidence that United States citizens use artifacts of the past to hold society together. The fact the exhibits connected to a restaurant was rather logical to the fixation on the past she observed across America: "You keep things in your homes from your ancestors; this is patriotic and keeps you more united. It's marvelous to keep the past."[36] This visitor couple reported seeing the material culture of the past in museums and homes from Alaska to Florida and remembered details of everything from rag rugs to taxidermy. Their impressions of the past in the United States were informed entirely by the history told in small museum exhibits and exhibits in non-museum settings.

While for the most part international visitors responded positively to small museums, several visitors indicated needs beyond those of English-speaking domestic visitors: language difficulties and a lack of a few key reference points. Visitors with English proficiency were probably more likely to fill out the survey (49 of 70 took the survey in English while 54 of 70 responded in English—the survey was available in English, French, German, Japanese, Spanish, and Chinese), making language difficulty less likely to appear in the survey, but a couple visitors indicated needing some assistance with English, such as one visitor's request for "subtitles please" on an introductory video. Other difficulties came from an interpretive approach that assumed audience training from the U.S. educational system and U.S. popular culture. One German visitor asked for "a short history lesson about this country's situation" during the U.S. Civil War so that he would have the backstory domestic visitors were more likely to have.

International and domestic visitors alike are drawn to some sites because of specialized interests. Da Yoopers Tourist Trap and Museum in rural northern Michigan has a rock shop with displays of the area's main industry: mining. Da Yoopers owner Jim DeCaire reports that the rock shop draws a number of visitors interested in geology and rock collecting who stay to explore the other exhibits on Upper Peninsula culture.[37] Four retirees interviewed at the vernacular exhibition on Chicago Cubs history in Murphy's Bleachers, a sports bar in Wrigleyville, were motivated by baseball history. They made baseball museums featured destinations in their travels, and saw their visit to Murphy's as a pilgrimage of sorts. They had been to the Negro Leagues Baseball Museum, the Little League World Series Museum, and the National Baseball Hall of Fame and Museum in Cooperstown, New York.[38] The sports bar that displayed Cubs artifacts was as important on their itinerary as the large museums.

The "authenticity" sought by tourists is the object of many a scholarly concern: concern for the environmental and cultural effects of tourism on the host country, concern that the history presented is too romantic, concern that corporate interests package history for consumption instead of thought.[39] Mostly what concerns visitors to exhibits in small museums and non-museum settings, however, is that they feel a *part* of the history, that they feel an emotional connection to a place and a people. The reality they encounter in exhibits is a constructed environment as well, as Dean MacCannell points out in his organization of tourist space into "front" and "back" zones of life for those presenting their culture to tourists.[40] However, in the small museum and non-museum setting, visitors are likely to come face-to-face with a representative of the history presented in the exhibit, which opens the opportunity for a more equal exchange than takes place in some of the more popular ethnographic performances aimed at tourists.

Scholars of museums have produced a great deal of work on identity performance and the ethnographic artifact.[41] These studies, however, typically focus on ethnographic objects managed by large, dominant culture institutions.[42] Scholarly overemphasis on the tourist gaze and the ethnographic performance of the visited, however, downplays the complicated dynamics of curator-visitor communication. The exchanges between curator and visitor in the small museum complicate the traditional ethnographic dichotomy between those doing the gazing and those being gazed upon, as well as the unequal power relationships traditionally informing the curator/visitor relationship. Because of the intimacy of the small museum setting, the visited gaze back. Outsiders become objects of curiosity for the visited just as the small museum curator—as living representative of the history on exhibit—is an object of curiosity for the tourist. The traditional curator's authority derives from scholarship, while the community curator's derives from a combination of scholarship, lived experience, the oral tradition, and identification with the community. The hybrid epistemology of private history exhibits complicates the traditional inequality between curator and visitor.

Visitors seek out small museums because of their interest in the "authentic," a collection of ideas of ethnic, regional, and cultural differences. Because of the intimacy of the private history exhibit, what they find instead are individuals who may or may not reflect fixed notions of group identity. At the same time, visitors as individuals represent their countries, ethnicities, and regions to curators in small U.S. museums. While this dynamic is often informed by differences in class (and therefore mobility), private history exhibits provide a great deal of opportunity for communication across boundaries. Visitors draw a diversity of conclusions from their visits. Shoshone-Bannock Tribal Museum manager Rosemary Devinney reports conversations with international visitors in which she senses their need to openly share feelings of anti-Americanism. A discussion of U.S. treatment of American Indians turns easily to contemporary U.S. foreign policy and actions. Devinney, a member of three nations (Shoshone, the Shoshone-Bannock nation created by the reservation system, and the United States) welcomes and encourages these conversations. Sometimes the conversations become even more personal. Olde Mill House Museum curator Jim Anderson reported that one 92-year-old repeat visitor admitted that Mr. Anderson was the first African American friend she ever had, and that he had helped her overcome a lifetime of prejudiced thinking.[43] Visitors may be motivated by an idea of "the authentic," but what they sometimes find, particularly in community and entrepreneurial exhibits but also in vernacular, are connections to individuals who can easily contradict preconceived notions about the groups to which the individuals belong.

Such intimacy is not the only reason visitors conceive of these exhibits as somehow more "real" than other experiences. Some museums are just so profoundly bizarre they could not have possibly made it through the market research faced by mass media cultural products, and it is this quirkiness that many visitors tend to equate with authenticity. Visitors' search for the "real" America—the one that is perceived to be managed by less glitzy technique, heavy production, and corporate sponsorship—can be found in discourse about a particular kind of museum: the "unusual museum," a descendent of the dime museum. While journalists had often covered the unusual museum, travel literature on these began springing up in the 1980s, with websites and blogs to follow. Jack Barth, Doug Kirby, Ken Smith, and Mike Wilkens published *Roadside America* in 1986, followed by a popular update in 1992: *The New Roadside America: The Modern Traveler's Guide to the Wild and Wonderful World of America's Tourist Attractions*. The authors place unusual museums in kitsch context, discussing them in the same terms as large balls of twine and Santa villages. Their chapter on historical museums asserts: "Most of us shy away from historical sites for the same reason we avoid dietetic candy and public television. If it doesn't sing, wiggle, or explode, why bother? . . . History is what we decide it should be, and it should be as loud, fast, and wiggly as possible."[44] The Confederama in Chattanooga, Tennessee, and Buckskin Joe's in Canon City, Colorado, are two that met their criteria, both museums they consider *not* politically correct. They criticize The Chinatown Tour (formerly the Chinese Opium Tunnel Museum) for "limp-wristed yuppification."[45] Joyce Jurnovoy and David Jenness's 1987 *America on Display: A Guide to Unusual Museums and Collections in the United States and Canada* takes a more folkloric approach and asserts the real North America could be found in unusual museums. The authors observed that "most of these unique repositories have evolved since 1970, as more cities and towns began to strive for cultural identity and to focus on the preservation of their grass roots traditions . . . . together they form a patchwork quilt, displaying so much of what's popular in America."[46] Whether because they lacked gentility or because they represented folk culture, unusual museums became more and more popular, as evidenced by significant blog activity on Roadside America's website, which debuted in 1996.[47] The increasing popularity of guides and websites on unusual museums coincided with the growth of the global economy and mass media exposure, attesting to visitors' search for quirkiness.

While the Roadside America phenomenon has spawned its own cyber community focused on the quirky, hobby shoppers were drawn to romanticized versions of history. Wilmington, North Carolina, produced a shopping center that uses artifacts to demonstrate the unbroken tradition of commerce in the port city, from cotton trade to hobby shopping, implying that being a shopper means being a part of an ongoing tradition. "The Cotton Exchange" is a popular downtown destination for tourists and locals alike. Its website asserts its meaning lies in the connection between past and present commerce:

> At the turn of the century, majestic sailing ships delivered treasures from around the world to the Port of Wilmington. Paddle-wheel boats plied the broad Cape Fear River from Southport to Fayetteville. Cotton was king, and one of the largest and busiest cotton export companies in the world was located in Wilmington. Today, The Cotton Exchange is still an adventure in trade.[48]

The site goes on to note that from this building, cotton went "to ports in Europe, England, and America" and explains the diversity of economic activity in the eight connected buildings before 1920: a Chinese laundry, a grocer, a barber, a seed company, a milling company, a "mariner's saloon,"

Figure 6.2. Automated teller machine at the center of a historical display of cotton's mercantile history. (The Cotton Exchange Shops and Restaurants, Historic Downtown, Wilmington, North Carolina, 2008. Photo by author.)

and a printing company. From there, the narrative skips to the buildings' restoration in 1975–1976, the first major effort in a downtown revitalization effort built largely on historic ambiance. Today, "special treasures, old-fashioned service, and a sense of history make *The Cotton Exchange* an exciting shopping adventure."[49] The Cotton Exchange includes photographic and artifact displays to give shoppers a sense of participating in the unbroken historical relationship to commerce. One display of an antique wagon, a bale of cotton, and a large painting of cotton merchants at work even includes a working ATM, allowing patrons access to cash and at the same time emphasizing the ongoing tradition of commerce.

The roughly thirty boutiques and restaurants of the contemporary Cotton Exchange are supported significantly by Wilmington's tourist economy, which has been carefully cultivated by investments in downtown revitalization and river front improvements. As did many cities in the United States starting in the 1960s and 70s, Wilmington sought to use its historic resources to build a tourist market. It has experienced significant success.[50] Museum-type displays have played a major role in this, and these displays connect with the cultural landscape evoked downtown, where one can ride on a paddleboat or tour mansions in a horse-drawn carriage.

While the history presented in The Cotton Exchange represents the role of cotton, mercantilism, and international exchange in the city's identity, it makes no mention of the race and class inequality upon which the economic system rested both before and after slavery. The history told in The Cotton Exchange is for contemporary shoppers who want to feel a part of a romantic history, instead of think about the social, political, and cultural effects of an economic system that exploited some and benefited others. The latter approach simply would not sell, which points out a significant problem in vernacular exhibitions that lack the face-to-face communication that allows visitors to see the history presented as an individualized perspective. Instead, the history presented has an institutional perspective, one visitors are less likely to question, therefore glossing over the historical inequalities that formed the basis of contemporary ones. One scholar has called this phenomenon, in the case of Detroit's Greektown, "the humiliation of history," the use of history to privilege those with expendable income seeking yet another themed environment in which to amuse themselves.[51]

While this assessment is certainly reasonable, it fails to capture other nuances of this cultural phenomenon, particularly in places—unlike The Cotton Exchange—in which the creators of the exhibits talk with visitors about history, therefore emphasizing the individualized perspective of the exhibits. In some sites, such as Murphy's Bleachers in Chicago and Ivar's in Seattle, patrons and workers alike felt that the artifacts connected them not just to the business that displayed them but to their larger communities of Wrigleyville and Seattle. It was through not only the exhibits that this was accomplished but through the conversations taking place among the exhibits. While the displays evoked a certain atmosphere for outsiders, they also served to make insiders feel closer to their communities.

In the first half of the decade 2000, the Ford Foundation and the organization Animating Democracy sponsored three projects significant to the study of history and intergroup dialogue. The Slave Galleries Restoration Project promoted dialogue about the history of race and class in Manhattan by bringing together representatives from diverse neighborhood groups to restore and plan tours of the slave galleries—rooms in which enslaved people worshipped at St. Augustine's Episcopal Church. Traces of the Trade was a community forum and documentary film project. The film followed one family's discovery of their ancestors' slave trading activities and provided the centerpiece for community discussions. The Without Sanctuary Project used an exhibit about lynching photography to host discussions of bigotry and violence. Public historian David Thelen, in his introduction to essays on the groundbreaking Animating Democracy projects, notes that "in all of these projects, the most thought-provoking dialogues seemed to arise when the situation combined familiarity and safety with the intriguing potential of differences in such a way that individuals did not feel compelled to identify with a single role or group."[52] His observation is an important one. The projects described were elaborate public history projects with multiple layers of community engagement, community education, facilitator training, films, tours, manuals, exhibits, and moderated conversations (to name a few). The results were profound. Participants reported major personal transformations on issues of racism and classism and meaningful community and intergroup dialogue. The positive effects of the projects are undeniable, but as three of the authors revealed, "dialogue is so resource intensive;"[53] these kinds of projects take significant expenditures in time, money, and professional expertise. The dialogue that takes place in many smaller exhibits among curators and visitors is not nearly as managed and its impact not as immediate or even as visible as the results of the Animating Democracy projects (although, in some cases it can be). However, history exhibits in small museums and in non-museum settings provide some of the groundwork for individuals to exchange ideas. Even if the curator or the visitor begins the conversation as a representative of a group, the intimacy of the setting tends to make curator and visitor alike more aware of the individuality in one another, the characteristic Thelen found to be so important to creating the high-impact dialogue present in the Animating Democracy case studies. When they emphasize face-to-face conversation with the individuals who created or are living with the legacy of this historical topic, private history exhibits have significant potential for creating dialogue. At their best, as at the Shoshone-Bannock Tribal Museum, private history exhibits facilitate meaningful conversations. At their worst, historical displays manipulate history simply to sell products.

Ultimately it is simply the presence of private history exhibits that make them an important phenomenon, for if they exist, they will inform visitors' uses of and expectations from professionalized exhibitions in larger, more formal museums. Whether they live up to the expectations of those in academic environments like museums and universities or not, private history exhibits affect visitors' understandings of the past. Therefore, they provide some general lessons for historical exhibition in more traditional exhibit settings in terms of exhibit design, programming, and content. First, visitors engage with the topic in settings that feel intimate, and this could be accomplished with a number of different design elements, such as breaking up large galleries into smaller spaces or mixing 2D design elements with folk art designs that represent or interpret the community being presented in the exhibit. Second, visitors like to converse, and programming could be designed to increase opportunities for visitors to talk with people who descend from the historical actors in an exhibit or who have spent a great deal of time thinking about how their ancestry informs their identity—encourage the elders, the genealogists, the first-hand witnesses to talk to visitors not just through technology but face-to-face. This does not mean giving up the authority of curatorial voice; rather, it means allowing visitors to consider multiple perspectives. Similarly, curatorial talks allow visitors to hear what it was like to research the topic and how it felt to explore the history. This emphasizes that exhibits are made by people, not simply institutions. Third, visitors to private history exhibits like to get up close and personal with artifacts, and as every living-history demonstrator knows, visitors like to try their hands. Visitors do not expect Disney-style, high-end immersion environments in private history exhibits and instead enjoy the real strengths of the small museum: people and artifacts that represent a unique place and perspective. No high-end immersions are necessary when curators truly trust their artifacts and their people, with all their qualities, flaws, and even eccentricities. Finally, most visitors just plain like hearing an honest delivery of history, even if it is unsettling, offensive, or gross. As scholars have asserted in reference to other historical media, nothing makes people lose interest in history quicker than the feeling that they're not getting the whole story.[54] If visitors get a story that only tells the genteel details of the topic, they know they are not getting the whole story. Visitors to history exhibits in diverse settings from diverse perspectives reveal that people really are interested in history, and it is that interest that can be the seed for growing better public dialogue on the past.

In his classic work on informal public space *The Great Good Place*, Ray Oldenburg concludes "the core settings of informal public life are as uniformly essential as they are outwardly variable."[55] If, as Oldenburg argues, informal gathering places are the core of community cohesion worldwide, then the private history exhibit in the United States has great potential as a "third place" of citizenships of all kinds: artisanal, ethnic, national, global. It is not just mobility, as Urry states, that should be a fundamental right of global citizenship, it is co-presence, the right to converse face-to-face with people from different countries, different communities.[56] The private history exhibit at its best, with its intimate galleries, its local relics, its multifunctional spaces, and its curators happy to converse, is a major contribution to dialogue among people separated by geographic and cultural distance.

The ultimate effects of the growth of historical exhibition are difficult to assess. In some ways these exhibits have popularized curation and restructured the authority of historical knowledge from that based on institutions to that based on a hybrid epistemology. In some cases, the history told is skewed, highly biased, or just plain not true, and, as James Loewen has theorized, historical "lies" perpetuate contemporary inequalities.[57] In other cases, though, the history presented brings strangers together to talk about personal, sometimes sensitive, topics. It is this last feature of exhibits in everyday spaces that is the most important: these exhibits provide the opportunity and the space for the beginnings of intergroup dialogue. While dialogue in the end is not transformative without action, it can provide a foundation for fuller participation in a democracy. The best private history exhibits collectively represent a broad attempt to replace the grand historical narrative not with bits and fragments of a fractured national history but with a fundamental belief in the necessity of intergroup dialogue to the survival of democracy.

Notes

CHAPTER ONE: HISTORICAL DISPLAY, COMMERCE, AND COMMUNITY

1. This is one of the communities so eloquently described by Robert R. Archibald in *The New Town Square: Museums and Communities in Transition* (Walnut Creek, CA: AltaMira Press, 2004).

2. Kenneth Ames, Barbara Franco, and L. Thomas Frye, eds., *Ideas and Images: Developing Interpretive History Exhibits* (Walnut Creek, CA: AltaMira Press, 1997); Steven C. Dubin, *Displays of Power: Controversy in the American Museum from the Enola Gay to Sensation* (New York: New York University Press, 1999); Mike Wallace, *Mickey Mouse History and Other Essays on American Memory* (Philadelphia: Temple University Press, 1996).

3. Mark Gottdiener, *The Theming of America: American Dreams, Media Fantasies, and Themed Environments* (Boulder, CO: Westview Press, 2001).

4. For examples, see John Dewey, *The Public and Its Problems* (Athens, OH and Chicago: Swallow Press, 1927 and 1954); Richard Sennett, *The Fall of Public Man* (New York: Knopf, 1977); and Jurgen Habermas, *The Structural Transformation of the Public Sphere* (Cambridge, MA: The MIY Press, 1989).

5. Art Carey, "Tony Polito Keeps a Cut Above: Sharing the Buzz with an Old School Barber," *Philadelphia Inquirer*, April 28, 2007.

6. Kathleen McLean, *Planning for People in Museum Exhibitions* (Washington, DC: Association of Science-Technology Centers, 1993), 115.

7. Jules David Prown, "The Truth of Material Culture: History or Fiction?" in Prown and Kenneth Haltman, *American Artifacts: Essays in Material Culture* (East Lansing: Michigan State University Press, 2000), 26.

8. Donna Haraway, "Situated Knowledges: The Science Question in Feminism and the Privilege of Partial Perspective," *Feminist Studies*, no. 3 (Fall 1988): 575–599.

9. Dixie Evans quoted by Michael Fleeman, "At Strippers' Museum, Reunion a Chance to Shed Not Only Clothes, But Old Myths," *The Charlotte Observer*, April 29, 1991.

10. Denise Meringolo provided insight on the development of the field in its academic and professional forms. In "Capturing the Public Imagination: The Social and Professional Place of Public History," *American Studies International* XLII, nos. 2 & 3 (June–October 2004), she writes that academicians provided definition to the field, which resulted in "a taxonomy of professionalism that locates public history beneath and perhaps to the right of university-driven historical scholarship." She calls for more scholarship on the nonacademic roots of the field. See also Marla R. Miller, "Playing to Strength: Teaching Public History at the Turn of the 21st Century," *American Studies International* XLII, nos. 2 & 3 (June–October 2004): 174–212; Deborah Welch, "Teaching Public History: Strategies for Undergraduate Program Development," *The Public Historian* 25, no. 1 (Winter 2003):71–82; and Constance B. Schulz, "An Academic Balancing Act: Public History Education Today," *The Public Historian* 21, no. 3 (Summer 1999):143–154.

11. G. Wesley Johnson, "The Origins of the Public Historian and the National Council on Public History," *The Public Historian* 21, no. 3 (Summer 1999): 175.

12. Michael Frisch, *A Shared Authority: Essays on the Craft and Meaning of Oral and Public History* (Albany: State University of New York Press, 1990).

13. The collection edited by Amy Levin is a recent, significant contribution to a literature that operates on a broadened definition of museums. See Amy Levin, ed, *Defining Memory: Local Museums and the Construction of History in America's Changing Communities*, (Lanham, MD: AltaMira Press, 2007).

14. The best work on the changes in the exhibition development process in history museums remains *Ideas and Images*. Kenneth Ames, Barbara Franco, and L. Thomas Frye, eds. *Ideas and Images: Developing Interpretive History Exhibits* (Walnut Creek, CA: AltaMira Press, 1992). Randolph Starn provides a comprehensive overview of recent literature in museum studies in "A Historian's Brief Guide to New Museum Studies," *American Historical Review* 110, no. 1 (February 2005): 68–98. For practice manuals, see Judy Diamond, *Practical Evaluation Guide: Tools for Museums and Other Informal Educational Settings* (Lanham, MD: AltaMira Press, 1999); Kathleen McLean, *Planning for People in Museum Exhibitions* (Washington, DC: Association of Science-Technology Centers, 1993); Beverly Serrell, *Exhibit Labels: An Interpretive Approach.* (Walnut Creek, CA: AltaMira Press, 1996). Leinhardt and Knutson studied visitor conversations in museums to demonstrate the diversity of interaction among visitors and exhibit elements. *Listening In on Museum Conversations.* (Walnut Creek, CA: AltaMira Press, 2004).

15. Christina Kreps, *Liberating Culture: Cross-Cultural Perspectives on Museums, Curation, and Heritage Preservation* (New York: Routledge, 2003). See also Eilean Hooper-Greenhill, *Museums and the Interpretation of Visual Culture* (New York: Routledge, 2000).

16. For discussions of the public engagement in exhibition development at large museums, see Steven C. Dubin, *Displays of Power: Controversy in the American Museum from the Enola Gay to Sensation* (New York: New York University Press, 1999); Mike Wallace, "The Battle of the Enola Gay" in *Mickey Mouse History and Other Essays on American Memory* (Philadelphia: Temple University Press, 1996); Victoria

Harden, "Museum Exhibit Standards: Do Historians Really Want Them?" *The Public Historian* 21, no. 3 (Summer 1999): 91–109.

17. Bella Dicks, *Culture on Display: The Production of Contemporary Visitability*, (Maidenhead, Berkshire, UK: Open University Press, 2003); Tony Bennett, *The Birth of the Museum: History, Theory, Politics* (New York: Routledge, 1995); David Lowenthal, *The Heritage Crusade and the Spoils of History* (Cambridge: Cambridge University Press, 1998); John Urry, *The Tourist Gaze: Leisure and Travel in Contemporary Societies* (London: Sage Publications, 1990).

18. Bennett, *Birth of the Museum*, 99, 73.

19. Dicks, *Culture on Display*, 134.

CHAPTER TWO: TOWARD A NEW TYPOLOGY OF HISTORICAL EXHIBITION IN THE UNITED STATES

An earlier version of this chapter appeared as "Heritage, Commerce and Museal Display: Toward a New Typology of Historical Exhibition in the United States," *The Public Historian* 30, no. 3 (2008): 27–50.

1. Kenneth Ames, Barbara Franco and L. Thomas Frye, eds., *Ideas and Images: Developing Interpretive History Exhibits* (Walnut Creek, CA: AltaMira, 1997); Mike Wallace, "Boat People: Immigrant History at the Statue of Liberty and Ellis Island," in *Mickey Mouse History and Other Essays on American Memory* (Philadelphia: Temple University Press, 1996), 55–73; Richard Handler and Eric Gable, *The New History in an Old Museum: Creating the Past at Colonial Williamsburg* (Durham and London: Duke University Press, 1997); Steven C. Dubin, *Displays of Power: Controversy in the American Museum from the Enola Gay to Sensation* (New York and London: New York University Press, 1999), 152–85.

2. *The Dead Sea Scrolls: Catalog of the Exhibition of Scrolls and Artifacts from the Collections of the Israel Antiquities Authority* (Grand Rapids, MI: Public Museum of Grand Rapids, 2003). www.grmuseum.org/exhibits/dead_sea_scrolls/images/navigation/exhibition.shtml (accessed January 20, 2006).

3. Claire Elderkin, "Coming of Age," *Museum News* (July/August 2005); Daniel Oliver, "From the Winners: 'Teen Chicago'," *Museum News* (September/October 2005). The development model used by the Chicago Historical Society reflects some of what Christina Kreps discusses as "indigenous curation," or the practice of preserving local traditions in the process of exhibition development. CHS's collaboration with teen researchers and curators is innovative in western professional practice, but certainly not new. It is somewhat similar to the Museum Balanga's (Indonesia) integration of religious specialists in their exhibition development for *The Art of Traditional Carving of Central Kalimantan*. Basirs, the carvers and keepers of religious knowledge associated with the carvings, made major curatorial choices and were assisted by the museum's curators, an inversion of traditional roles in the ethnographic museum. Local knowledge was fundamental to interpretation. See Christina Kreps, *Liberating Culture: Cross Cultural Perspectives on Museums, Curation, and Heritage Preservation*, (New York: Routledge, 2003), 29–34.

4. Palace of the Governors, Santa Fe, New Mexico, April 13, 2007. This institution is currently undergoing radical changes. See Tammy S. Gordon, "Palace of the Governors," *The Public Historian* 29, no. 4 (Fall 2007): 91–93.

5. *Without Sanctuary: Lynching Photography in America,* Charles H. Wright Museum of African American History, Detroit, Michigan, August 25, 2004.

6. *Without Sanctuary.*

7. Victor Danilov, *A Planning Guide for Corporate Museums, Galleries, and Visitor Centers* (New York: Greenwood Press, 1992), 4.

8. Danilov, *A Planning Guide,* 5.

9. The History Factory. www.historyfactory.com/index.aspx?sectionid=23 (accessed April 25, 2007).

10. In addition to the planning guide cited above, Danilov authored *Corporate Museums, Galleries, and Visitor Centers: A Directory* (Westport, CT: Greenwood Press, 1991), which includes descriptions of 329 corporate museums in 16 countries.

11. Mark Rectanus, *Culture Incorporated: Museums, Artists, and Corporate Sponsorships,* (Minneapolis: University of Minnesota Press, 2002).

12. Neil Harris' review of The World of Coca-Cola is a particularly effective one. Neil Harris, "The World of Coca-Cola," *The Journal of American History* 82, no. 1 (June 1995): 154–158.

13. Ted Friedman, "The World of *The World of Coca-Cola,*" *Communication Research* 19, no. 5 (October 1992): 642–662.

14. Harris, "The World of Coca-Cola," 157.

15. This discussion of The World of Coca-Cola is based on visits to the museum in the mid-1990s. In May of 2007, the museum opened new and revised exhibits. The museum website describes the changes as such: "Our new and expanded World has something for everyone!

Thrilling 4-D Theater
World's largest collection of Coke memorabilia
Fully functioning bottling line that produces commemorative 8-ounce bottles of Coca-
    Cola®
Tasting experience with over 70 different products to sample
Pop Culture Gallery featuring works by artists such as Andy Warhol, Norman Rockwell,
    and Steve Penley
World-famous CocaCola® Polar Bear
And so much more!

It's the only place where you can explore the complete story—past, present, and future—of the world's best-known brand!" www.woccatlanta.com/ (accessed May 22, 2007).

16. Margot A. Wallace, *Museum Branding: How to Create and Maintain Image, Loyalty, and Support* (Lanham, MD: AltaMira Press, 2006). See also Jennifer Deutsch, *Just Who Do Your Customers Think You Are?: A Guide to Branding Your Organization,* (Lansing,MI: Michigan Museums Association, 2002).

17. Jennifer Eichstedt and Stephen Small, *Representations of Slavery: Race and Ideology in Southern Plantation Museums* (Washington, DC and London: Smithsonian Institution Press, 2002); James Loewen, *Lies Across America: What Our Historic Sites Get Wrong* (New York: Simon and Schuster, 1999).

18. Amy Levin, ed. *Defining Memory: Local Museums and the Construction of History in America's Changing Communities* (Lanham, MD: AltaMira Press, 2007). See also Ron Chew, "In Praise of the Small Museum," *Museum News* (March/April 2002): 37–41.

19. "A Century of History," Hebrew Union Congregation, Greenville, Mississippi. www.hebrewunion.org/study/adults/ (accessed January 2, 2008).

20. Jim Anderson, interview by author, videorecording, Homosassa, Florida, June 10, 2006.

21. Visitor Interview B3, Olde Mill House Printing Museum, June 9, 2006.

22. Middlefield Cheese Museum, Middlefield, Ohio, June 17, 2005.

23. Saul Rubin, *Offbeat Museums: The Collections and Curators of America's Most Unusual Museums* (Santa Monica, CA: Santa Monica Press, 1997), 150–153; John McVey, "The American Sanitary Plumbing Museum: Unusual Exhibit Features the Fixtures at the Business End of the Pipe," *The Lay of the Land: The Center for Land Use Interpretation Newsletter* (Spring 1997). www.clui.org/clui_4_1/lotl/lotlv10/sanitary. html (accessed April 30, 2007).

24. These settings are described by Oldenburg as the "third place," the one between work and home that provides opportunity or significant community cohesion. Ray Oldenburg, *The Great Good Place: Cafes, Coffee Shops, Bookstores, Bars, Hair Salons and Other Hangouts at the Heart of a Community* (New York: Marlowe and Company, 1989, 1997, 1999).

25. Visitor interviews at Murphy's Bleachers, Chicago, Illinois, June 27–28, 2006.

26. Kurt Dewhurst and Marsha MacDowell, "Museum for the People: Museum Bars," *Material Culture* 18, no. 1 (Spring 1986): 37–49.

27. Alan Beardsworth and Alan Bryman, "Late Modernity and the Dynamics of Quasification," *The Sociological Review*: 47, no. 2 (1999): 240.

28. The following document a variety of exhibitions, including vernacular exhibits: Christine Des Garennes, *Great Little Museums of the Midwest* (Black Earth, WI: Trails Books, 2002); Joyce Jurnovoy and David Jenness, *America On Display: A Guide to Unusual Museums and Collections in the United States and Canada* (New York: Facts on File Publications, 1987); Saul Rubin, *Offbeat Museums*; and Mike Wilkins, Ken Smith, and Doug Kirby, *The New Roadside America: The Modern Traveler's Guide to the Wild and Wonderful World of America's Tourist Attractions* (New York: Simon and Schuster, 1992).

29. Menu, B&J's American Café, July 8, 2005.

30. *Liberty Antiques Mall*, Dewitt, Michigan, July 9, 2004.

31. Conversations with patrons at the Euclid Avenue Yacht Club, Atlanta, Georgia, April 13, 2006.

32. Andrew Pekarik recently wrote of the problem of outcome-based evaluation in the context of interactives development. See "Engineering Answers," *Curator: The Museum Journal* 47, no. 2: 145–148.

33. George Hein presents a useful summary overview in chapters 3 and 4 of *Learning in the Museum* (New York: Routledge, 1998). For a discussion of early visitor studies, see Kenneth Hudson, *A Social History of Museums: What the Visitors Thought* (Atlantic Highlands, NJ: Humanities Press, 1975).

34. Visitor Interview A6, Da Yoopers Tourist Trap and Museum, Ishpeming, Michigan, May 24, 2006.

CHAPTER THREE: COMMUNITY EXHIBITION:
HISTORY, IDENTITY, AND DIALOGUE

1. Marcia G. Synnott, "Hugh Macrae, Penderlea, and the Model Farm Communities Movement," *Proceedings of the South Carolina Historical Association* (1987): 53–65; Ann S. Cottle, *The Roots of Penderlea: A Memoir of a New Deal Homestead Community* (Winston-Salem, NC: John F. Blair, 2008); Penderlea Homestead Museum. http://www.penderleahomesteadmuseum.org/ (accessed February 16, 2009).

2. Ann Cottle quoted in Renee Gannon, "Growing Up on Penderlea," *Carolina Country.* http://www.carolinacountry.com/StoryPages/ourstories/penderlea/Penderlea2.07.pdf

3. Nick Stanley, *Being Ourselves for You: The Global Display of Cultures* (London: Middlesex University Press, 1998), 87–97; Sidney Moko Mead, "Indigenous Models of Museums in Oceania," *Museum* 35, no. 139 (1983): 98–101.

4. Christina Kreps, *Liberating Culture: Cross Cultural Perspectives on Museums, Heritage, Curation, and Heritage Preservation* (New York: Routledge, 2003), 34–45.

5. Amy Levin, "Nostalgia As Epistemology," in *Defining Memory: Local Museums and the Construction of History in America's Changing Communities* (Lanham, MD: Alta Mira, 2007), 94. See also in *Defining Memory*: Jay Price, "The Small Town We Never Were: Old Cowtown Museum Faces an Urban Past", 97–108; Stuart Patterson, "'The Dream Then and Now': Democratic Nostalgia and the Living Museum at Arthurdale, West Virginia", 109–126; and Heather R. Perry, "History Lessons: Selling the John Dillinger Museum", 127–142.

6. For a discussion of world's fair display, see Barbara Kirshenblatt-Gimblett, *Destination Culture: Tourism, Museums, and Heritage* (Berkeley: University of California Press, 1998); and John G. Cawelti, "America on Display: The World's Fairs of 1876, 1893, 1933" in Frederic Cople Jaher, ed., *The Age of Industrialism in America: Essays in Social Structure and Cultural Values* (New York: The Free Press, 1968), 317–363.

7. Carol Kammen, *On Doing Local History*, 2nd ed., (Walnut Creek, CA: AltaMira Press, 2003), 12–15.

8. Patricia West, *Domesticating History: The Political Origins of America's House Museums* (Washington, DC: Smithsonian Institution Press, 1999), 39–43. Laurel Thatcher Ulrich provides a rich analysis of the relationship between colonial history and antebellum New Englanders' identification with its artifacts. See *The Age of Homespun: Objects and Stories in the Creation of an American Myth* (New York: Vintage Books, 2001).

9. Kirschenblatt-Gimblett, *Destination Culture*, 17–78; West, *Domesticating History*, 40.

10. David J. Russo, *Keepers of Our Past: Local Historical Writing in the United States, 1820s-1930s* (New York: Greenwood Press, 1988), 195.

11. Russo, *Keepers*, 197; Kammen, *On Doing Local History*, 34. For more on the split among amateurs and professionals in the American Historical Association, see Peter Novick, *That Noble Dream: The "Objectivity Question" and the American Historical Profession* (Cambridge: Cambridge University Press, 1988), 193–195.

12. Denise Meringolo, "Capturing the Public Imagination: The Social and Professional Place of Public History," *American Studies International* 42, nos. 2 & 3 (June–October 2004): 95.

13. Meringolo, "Capturing the Public Imagination," 97.
14. Kammen, *On Doing Local History*, 30–31.
15. Kammen, *On Doing Local History*, 36.
16. As Peter Novick has shown, even within academic circles objectivity is a highly contested concept.
17. Two hundred surveys were sent to small history museums in the fall of 2006. The sample was compiled from Lynne Arany and Archie Hobson, *Little Museums: Over 1,000 Small and Not-so-Small American Showplaces* (New York: H. Holt, 1998); Lois Buttlar and Lubomyr Roman Wynar, *Guide to Information Resources in Ethnic Museum, Library, and Archival Collections in the United States* (Westport, CT: Greenwood Press, 1996); "Historical Museum Guide to the United States." http://www.censusfinder.com/guide_to_historical_museums.htm (accessed September 2006).
18. Kammen, *On Doing Local History*, 61.
19. Rachel Travers, "House Tour is More Than They Bargained For," *The Boston Globe*, September 27, 2001, H3.
20. Virginia Culver, "'Mr. Delta' Gave His All for Town and Museum," *The Denver Post*, July 9, 2006, C-06.
21. Matt Baron, "'Driving Force' in Historical Society Keeps Pedal to Metal," *Chicago Tribune*, March 10, 2004.
22. Sylvia Brenner, "Having Blast With the Past: N.M. Curator Loves Slower Pace," *The Denver Post*, February 12, 2000, A-26.
23. Fort Hall Business Council, *Shoshone-Bannock Tribes: Fort Hall, Idaho* brochure, 1988–89. Shoshone-Bannock Tribal Museum.
24. Shoshone-Bannock Tribal Enterprises, Trading Post Complex. http://www.sho-ban.com/trade/htm (accessed May 23, 2005).
25. Rosemary Devinney, interview by author, videorecording, Fort Hall, Idaho, July 12, 2006. Museum Assistant April Eschief also reported being asked about living in teepees. April Eschief, interview by author, videorecording, Fort Hall, Idaho, July 14, 2006.
26. Delbert Farmer, interview by author, videorecording, Fort Hall, Idaho, July 14, 2006. Rusty Houtz, interview by author, videorecording, Fort Hall, Idaho, July 12, 2006. Rosemary Devinney, in her interview, described the differences in the tours these two men give.
27. Devinney interview, July 14, 2006.
28. Devinney interview, July 14, 2006.
29. Devinney interview, July 14, 2006.
30. Rusty Houtz, Delbert Farmer, and Rosemary Devinney interviews.
31. *Woodenware*. Alger County Heritage Center, Munising, Michigan, August 10, 2004.
32. Needs Assessment Survey Response, November 2006. In possession of author.
33. Kelly Westhoff, "Donaldsville, Louisiana: A Road Trip Back in Time," GoNomad. http://www.gonomad.com/destinations/0808/louisiana-donaldson.html (accessed February 16, 2009).
34. The growth of small museums on African American history has paralleled the rise of larger museums dedicated to the subject since the 1960s. See Tilden Rhea, *Race Pride and the American Identity* (Cambridge: Harvard University Press, 1997), particularly 94–123; Patricia West's chapter on Booker T. Washington's birthplace in

Domesticating History: The Political Origins of America's House Museums (Washington, DC: Smithsonian Institution Press, 1999), 129–157; Eichstedt and Small discuss "counter narratives," interpretations of slavery from "Black-centric" perspectives in *Representations of Slavery: Race and Ideology in Southern Plantation Museums* (Washington, DC and London: Smithsonian Institution Press, 2002), 233–256. They describe a visit to the River Road African American Museum on pages 250–254.

35. Charles Broadwell, "200-Year-Old Church to Celebrate in Style," *The Fayetteville Observer*, October 1, 1992.

36. "50 Years of Worship," *Houston Chronicle*, September 9, 2004. Newsbank. See also Cay Fultz, "High Street Church to Hold Homecoming," *Richmond Times-Dispatch*, September 19, 1990; Lisa Bellamy, "Bit By Bit, Church Builds to a Celebration: First Presbyterian Prepares for its 175th Anniversary," *The News and Observer*, January 10, 1991.

37. Christine Temin, "A Daring Sanctuary For Art," *Boston Globe*, January 13, 1983.

38. Hebrew Union Congregation's "Century of History." http://www.hebrewunion .org/study/adults/ (accessed December 27, 2007).

39. Beth Ahabah Museum and Archives. http://www.bethahabah.org/bama/ index.htm (accessed December 27, 2007). See also Alberta Lindsey, "A Rich Heritage: Jews in Richmond, Nation Mark 350th Anniversary of Judaism in America," *Richmond Times-Dispatch*, December 4, 2004.

40. Belle Gunness Exhibit, LaPorte Historical Society Museum, LaPorte, Indiana, July 8, 2005; "Belle Gunness, LaPorte's 'Lady Bluebeard,'" LaPorte Historical Society. http://laportecountyhistory.org/belleg1.htm (accessed May 17, 2007).

41. Belle Gunness Exhibit.

42. Susie Richter, e-mail message to author, November 28, 2007.

43. Nancy Maes, "Some Real-Life Events Turn Into Scary Legends as Years Slither By," *Chicago Tribune*, October 24, 1997.

44. See Jennifer Eichstedt and Stephen Small, *Representations of Slavery: Race and Ideology in Southern Plantation Museums* (Washington, DC and London: Smithsonian Institution Press, 2002).

45. Ghost Walk of Old Wilmington, Wilmington, North Carolina, Fall 2005; Ryan Dougherty, "Haunting History," *National Parks* 77, no. 9 (September 2003).

46. Nancy Fike quoted in Maes, "Real-Life Events."

47. Thomas Blom explores the connection between the media and the appeal of "morbid tourism." See "Morbid Tourism: A Postmodern Market Niche with an Example from Althorp," *Norwegian Journal of Geography*, 54 no. 1 (2001): 29–36.

48. Roy Rosenzweig and David Thelen, *The Presence of the Past: Popular Uses of History in American Life* (New York: Columbia University Press, 1998), 120–121.

49. Billy Sunday Visitors Center, Winona Lake, Indiana, July 9, 2005.

50. Billy Sunday Visitors Center, Winona Lake, Indiana, July 9, 2005.

51. Bruce Davis quoted in Devra First, "9,000 Square Feet, 26 Rooms, 1 Guy: His Home Not Only Houses 27 Collections, It's a Collector's Item Itself," *The Boston Globe*, May 13, 2004, H1.

52. Catherine Bowman, "Where Pop Icons Go to Die," *The San Francisco Chronicle*, January 23, 1989, A3.

53. Paul Liberatore, "Unknown Museum Lives On, Privately," *Marin Independent Journal*, April 3, 2006. http:www.marinjj.com/millvalley/ci_3668565 (accessed December 26, 2007).

54. McGowan quoted in Liberatore, "Unknown Museum."

55. As some scholars have noted, the term "media saturation" usually refers to the amount of media and not its particular characteristics. However, cultural products in media-saturated cultures are highly refined and managed due to the competition provided by their commonality and abundance. See Jay Newell, "Revisiting Schramm's Radiotown: Media Displacement and Saturation," *Journal of Radio Studies* 14, no. 1: 3–19; John Sherry, "Media Saturation and Entertainment-Education," *Communication Theory* 12, no. 2 (May 2002): 206–224; and Todd Gitlin, *Media Unlimited: How the Torrent of Images and Sounds Overwhelms Our Lives* (New York: Metropolitan Books, 2001).

56. While Stanley's work is primarily in contemporary ethnographic display, history exhibits by indigenous curators are within this realm, especially when, as is the case with many indigenous exhibits, the curators are present in the gallery to engage visitors in conversation. As "authentic" products of the history being displayed, they become representatives of that past.

57. In addition to work already cited by Bella Dicks and Barbara Kirshenblatt-Gimblett, see Michael Ames, *Cannibal Tours and Glass Boxes: The Anthropology of Museums* (Vancouver and Toronto: UBC Press, 1992); Steven C. Dubin, *Displays of Power: Controversy in the American Museum from the Enola Gay to Sensation* (New York: New York University Press, 1999); and Moira G. Simpson, *Making Representations: Museums in the Post-Colonial Era* (London and New York: Routledge, 1996).

58. This discussion is based on extended, recorded interviews with four staff members/volunteers and twenty-six exit interviews with visitors to the Shoshone-Bannock Tribal Museum, conducted during July 2006. The visitor interviews were face-to-face, with open-ended questions and a demographic information card. Conducted with individual visitors from different visitor groups. Conducted July 11–15 between 9:50 a.m. and 5:00 p.m. They were part of visitor groups totaling sixty-four people. The average number for visitor groups was 2.46.

59. Delbert Farmer interview.

60. Visitor surveys, Shoshone-Bannock Tribal Museum, July 11–15, 2006.

61. Conversations observed by author in lobby of Shoshone-Bannock Tribal Museum, July 11-15, 2006.

62. Needs Assessment Survey, Fall 2006, in possession of author.

63. Needs Assessment Survey.

64. "Self-Guided Tour of IXL Historical Museum," IXL Museum, May 2006. The author wishes to thank Laurie Riedy, Museum Manager, for sharing guide materials.

CHAPTER FOUR: ENTREPRENEURIAL EXHIBITION:
HISTORICAL DISPLAY AND THE SMALL BUSINESS TRADITION

1. "Firefighters Museum Finds a Home in Shopping Mall," *St. Louis Post Dispatch*, September 4, 2006.

2. "Review of Hazelwood (St. Louis), Missouri, First Due Fire Museum." roadsideamerica.com (accessed September 3, 2007).

3. First Due Fire Museum. www.firstduefiremuseum.com/services.html (accessed September 3, 2007).

4. Mansel G. Blackford provides an excellent overview of the history of small business. He asserts that business historians have privileged large enterprise because it effected the most drastic changes in business practice. However, the study of small business provides insight into continuing cultural views of the small-business person as the backbone of American enterprise. He also demonstrates the continuing small business tradition of serving specialty markets. Mansel G. Blackford, *A History of Small Business in America*, 2nd ed., (Chapel Hill and London: University of North Carolina Press, 2003). Jonathan J. Bean provides an overview of mid-twentieth-century legislation affecting small businesses. Jonathan J. Bean, *Beyond the Broker State: Federal Policies Toward Small Business, 1936–1961* (Chapel Hill and London: University of North Carolina Press, 1996).

5. Michele Lamont, *The Dignity of Working Men: Morality and the Boundaries of Race, Class and Immigration* (Cambridge: Harvard University Press, 2000), 22.

6. Tom Shactman's *Around the Block: The Business of a Neighborhood* examines the people involved in small business and provides an in-depth look at their significance in community life (New York: Harcourt Brace, 1997). For historical background on the formation of artisanal and middle classes in the United States, see Sean Wilentz, *Chants Democratic: New York City and the Rise of the American Working Class, 1788–1850* (New York and Oxford: Oxford University Press, 1984); and Stuart Blumin, *The Emergence of the Middle Class: Social Experience in the American City, 1760–1900* (Cambridge: Cambridge University Press, 1989).

7. Richard Florida, *The Rise of the Creative Class and How It's Transforming Work, Leisure, Community and Everyday Life* (New York: Basic Books, 2000); Michael Piore, "The Reconfiguration of Work and Employment Relations in the United States at the Turn of the Century," *Advances in Life Course Research* 8: 23–44. Piore further suggests that the current system suppresses economic identities based on trade or profession and encourages governmental regulation of workplaces around racial, gendered or ability identities.

8. Jennifer Olvera, "Special Museums Give Guests a Dose of Career Counseling," *Chicago Tribune*, November 5, 2004.

9. Robert Carroll, "Satisfaction in Serving Those in Grief," *The Boston Globe*, May 4, 2006.

10. David Pittman, "Museum Examines History of Pharmacy," *Amarillo Globe-News*, March 8, 2007.

11. David Blackburn, "Exhibit Highlights Nurses' History: Items on Display in Independence Bank Lobby," *Messenger-Inquirer* (Owensboro, KY), May 20, 2006.

12. The Freakatorium: El Museo Loco, www.freakatorium.com/events.html (accessed October 1, 2007).

13. Dixie Evans quoted by Saul Rubin, *Offbeat Museums: The Collections and Curators of America's Most Unusual Museums*, (Santa Monica, CA: Santa Monica Press, 1997), 223. Anne Fliotsos asserts burlesque lost any remaining claim to respectability by the 1920s when it "had degenerated to little more than raunchy jokes and striptease." "Gotta Get a Gimmick: The Burlesque Career of Millie De Leon," *Journal of American Culture* 21, no. 4 (Winter 1998): 1–8. For insight on burlesque dancers as workers see Leigh Ann Wheeler, "Battling Over Burlesque: Conflicts Between

Maternalism, Paternalism, and Organized Labor, 1920–1932," *Frontiers: A Journal of Women Studies* 20, no. 2 (1999): 148–74.

14. James Sullivan, "Burlesque Shows Still Alive and Kicking," *The San Francisco Chronicle*, September 26, 2002.

15. Michael Lewis quoted in Rob Young, "Museum Gets New Life—Partnership with ECU Helps Celebrate Rural Medicine's Roots," *The Daily Reflector* (Greenville, NC), April 15, 2004. Lewis's evocation of the country doctor had particular resonance for the South, where doctors were known to have particularly strong connections to the community. See Steven Stowe, *Doctoring the South: Southern Physicians and Everyday Medicine in the Mid-Nineteenth Century* (Chapel Hill: University of North Carolina Press, 2004).

16. Lynn Setzer, "House Calls and Herbal Remedies," *The News and Observer* (Raleigh, NC), February 22, 2001.

17. Sarah Avery, "Country Doctor Museum Will Make You Queasy," *The News and Observer*, July 9, 2007.

18. Julia Keller, "Sawbones Central," *Chicago Tribune*, August 17, 2005.

19. Andrew Hermann, "Museum's Bloody Good Show," *Chicago Sun-Times*, May 3, 2007.

20. Neil Steinberg, "Miracles of Not-So-Modern Medicine," *Chicago Sun-Times*, May 18, 2000.

21. Rubin, *Offbeat Museums*, 226–29.

22. Associated Press, "Community-Based Mental Health Treatment Replaces Long Hospital Stays," *St. Louis Post Dispatch*, July 18, 1999.

23. William Childress, "Dignity for the Mentally Ill," *St. Louis Post-Dispatch*, June 5, 1993.

24. Amy Lignitz, "Some Will Mind Horrors of Psychiatric Museum/Brutality, Ignorance in Times Past on Display," *Houston Chronicle*, December 4, 1994.

25. Amy Lignitz, "Some Will Mind."

26. Tanya S. Blank, "Bragg Touts 2 Museums," *The Fayetteville Observer*, August 24, 2000.

27. Lynn Setzer, "The Road to Special Warfare," *The News and Observer*, November 1, 2001.

28. Posting by "neela," *Hyphen: Asian America Unabridged.* www.hyphenmagazine .com/blog/archives/2005/11/tule_lake_at_th.html (accessed October 9, 2007).

29. Associated Press, "Border Patrol Store Drops Racist T-Shirt," *Boston Globe*, January 13, 1989.

30. "Visitors May Get Longer Look at Farming of Yesteryear." Washington County Fair, Greenwich, New York. www.washingtoncountyfair.com/museum.htm (accessed October 31, 2007).

31. "Pioneering Spirit Lives on in Elementary School Program," *The Seattle Times*, April 11, 2001.

32. William Hageman, "Ox-Handling Class at Museum Smells Like Team Spirit," *Chicago Tribune*, May 24, 2005.

33. Karen Goldberg Goff, "Eking Out a Living," *The Washington Times*, August 22, 2004.

34. "Laid Off Worker Fires Up Career in Reading, Pa. Iron Trade," *Reading Eagle*, April 29, 2002. McDaniel's book is *A Blacksmithing Primer: A Course in Basic and Intermediate Blacksmithing*. It is self-published and available at www.drgnfly4g.com/ (accessed October 31, 2007).

35. Beth Gauper, "Hardy Marquette: U.P. Town Holds on to its Rustic Persona in the Midst of Creeping Sophistication," *Chicago Tribune*, January 11, 1998. Robert R. Archibald provides interesting perspectives on Ishpeming in his study of place and public history, *The New Town Square: Museums and Communities in Transition* (Walnut Creek, CA: AltaMira Press, 2004).

36. "Yooper Innovation," Da Yoopers Tourist Trap and Museum, Ishpeming, Michigan, August 2004.

37. Jim DeCaire, interview by author, videorecording, Ishpeming, Michigan, May 26, 2006.

38. Bella Dicks, *Culture on Display: The Production of Contemporary Visitability* (Maidenhead, Berkshire, UK: Open University Press, 2003), 138; see also Barbara Kirshenblatt-Gimblett, *Destination Culture: Tourism, Museums, and Heritage* (Berkeley: University of California Press, 1998); and John Urry, *The Tourist Gaze: Leisure and Travel in Contemporary Societies* (London: Sage Publications, 1990).

39. Jim DeCaire, interview by author, May 26, 2006.

40. Visitor interview A19, May 26, 2006.

41. Ray Sharp quoted in "Michigan Partnership Boosts MIChild Enrollment," *Sound Partners for Community Health* website. www.soundpartners.org/node/1672 (accessed October 9, 2006).

42. Charlie Gere, *Digital Culture* (London: Reaktion Books, 2002). See also Mark Poster, *Information Please: Culture and Politics in the Age of Digital Machines* (Durham and London: Duke University Press, 2006); and Lauren Rabinovitz and Abraham Geil, eds., *Memory Bytes: History, Technology, and Digital Culture* (Durham and London: Duke University Press, 2004).

43. Florida Secrets. www.floridasecrets.com/Restaurants/WC/MuseumCafe.htm (accessed January 31, 2006).

44. Jim Anderson, interview by author, videorecording, Homosassa, Florida, June 10, 2006.

45. While Mr. Anderson prefers the term "negro" for self-identification, I use "African American" here because it is standard usage. He explains his preference for "negro" in terms of his close identification with Florida, its land and culture, and the enslaved people who used to work the nearby sugar mill. James Anderson, interview by author, videorecording, Homosassa, Florida, June 10, 2006.

46. James Anderson, interview by author, videorecording, Homosassa, Florida, June 10, 2006.

47. Interviews with visitors were conducted over two to four day visits to these museums in May, June, and July of 2006. The interviews consisted of face-to-face, open-ended questions recorded by the author as well as a demographic survey card filled out by visitors.

48. Visitor interview B3, Homosassa, Florida, June 9, 2006. Another reported "It's amazing how they started out . . . like when Jim demonstrates the machines and to think of a hundred years ago. Jim is very charming." Visitor interview B7, Homosassa, Florida, June 10, 2006.

49. Anderson interview.
50. Anderson interview.
51. Anderson interview.
52. Anderson interview.

CHAPTER FIVE: VERNACULAR EXHIBITION AND THE BUSINESS OF HISTORY

1. Introductory label, Ivar's Acres of Clams, January 7, 2005.

2. "What Makes Ivar's Famous," Ivar's Acres of Clams Employee Manual, January, 2005; Paul Dorpat, "Haglund, Ivar (1905–1985)," HistoryLink.org: The Online Encyclopedia of Washington State University. historylink.org (accessed January 7, 2005).

3. Richard Handler and Eric Gable, *The New History in an Old Museum: Creating the Past at Colonial Williamsburg* (Durham and London: Duke University Press, 1997), 37–39. See also Mark Rectanus, *Culture Incorporated: Museums, Artists, and Corporate Sponsorships* (Minneapolis: University of Minnesota Press, 2002).

4. Jerry Herron, *AfterCulture: Detroit and the Humiliation of History* (Detroit: Wayne State University Press, 1993), 18–21.

5. Jakle and Sculle explore national food marketing as governed by "total design," which emphasizes predictable formulae. See John. A. Jakle and Keith A. Sculle, *Fast Food: Roadside Restaurants in the Automobile Age* (Baltimore and London: The Johns Hopkins University Press, 1999); and Richard Pillsbury, *No Foreign Food: The American Diet in Time and Place* (Boulder, CO: Westview Press, 1998). For franchising history and contemporary practices, see Stan Luxenberg, *Roadside Empires: How the Chains Franchised America* (New York: Viking Penguin, 1985).

6. See Jakle and Sculle, *Fast Food*, 20–93; and Luxenberg, *Roadside Empires*, 12–30. See also Harvey Levenstein, *Paradox of Plenty: A Social History of Eating in Modern America* (New York: Oxford University Press, 1993), 40–49.

7. Jakle and Sculle, *Fast Food*, 217–219

8. Jakle and Sculle, *Fast Food*, 271–272.

9. Jakle and Sculle, *Fast Food*, 288.

10. Press coverage did not employ the term "sports bar" until Champions started using the tag line "The Ultimate Sports Bar" in the early 1980s.

11. Mike O'Harro quoted in Mariah Burton Nelson, "Unsung Pioneers: Sometimes There's No First Place Trophy," *The Leadership Game: Washington Business Journal.* mariahburtonnelson.com (accessed June 19, 2007).

12. Rudy Maxa, "Confessions of a Don Juan," *Washington Post Magazine*, February 13, 1983. In his interview with Maxa, the 43-year-old O'Harro bragged he preferred to date women between 18 and 20, stating "I like a girl who is an uncut diamond—one I can cut and polish." He held on to this persona even after four members of the Washington Capitals were accused of raping and sodomizing a 17-year-old girl in one of the limousines his bar provided the players to get them to and from Champions for a team party. The players were cleared of charges. "I'm sorry for the young lady and for the players, but now that it is over I would not

hesitate having parties for any team . . . . I think [the incident] was blown way out of proportion." O'Harro quoted in Karen Goldberg, "Sports Bar Owners Relieved Capitals Were Cleared," *Washington Times*, July 2, 1990.

13. Ballard, *Sports Illustrated* via Academic Search Premier; Burton Nelson, "Unsung Pioneers"; and Jeffrey Yorke, "Champions in Georgetown: Providing a Sporting Chance," *Washington Post*, December 30, 1983.

14. Yorke, "Champions in Georgetown."

15. Rick Vaughn quoted in Yorke, "Champions in Georgetown."

16. Chuck Conconi, "O.J. on the Town," *Washington Post*, November 7, 1984.

17. Eve Zibart, "Sporting Companions," *Washington Post*, July 10, 1992.

18. Ballard, *Sports Illustrated* via Academic Search Premier.

19. Craig Wolff, "Pieces of Sport Fantasy Fetch High Prices in the Real World," *New York Times*, August 20, 1989. John Leptich, "Mays, Mantle Artwork Hanging on Local Wall," *Chicago Tribune*, October 16, 1989. O'Harro was not new to the museum formats. In 1984 he loaned his science fiction memorabilia to the National Museum of American History for the exhibit "Yesterday's Tomorrow's: Past Visions of the American Future." Joe Brown, "Rocket Man," *Washington Post*, September 12, 1984.

20. Ballard, *Sports Illustrated* via Academic Search Premier.

21. Harvey Levenstein, *Paradox of Plenty: A Social History of Eating in Modern America* (New York: Oxford University Press, 1993), 40–49.

22. John Galvin, "Making the World Safe for Miller Lite," *New York Times Magazine*, October 18, 1998, 90.

23. Robert Hollands and Paul Chatterton, "Producing Nightlife in the New Urban Entertainment Economy: Corporatization, Branding and Market Segmentation," *International Journal of Urban and Regional Research* 27, no. 2 (June 2003): 361.

24. Emil's menu front, September 2004. In possession of author.

25. Upper Peninsula Sports Hall of Fame, Iron Mountain, Michigan, May 2004.

26. Euclid Avenue Yacht Club, April 2006. "Euclid Avenue Yacht Club-Atlanta, GA, 30307-1939-Citysearch." atlanta.citysearch.com/profile/2998216 (accessed April 12, 2006).

27. Interviews with patrons, Euclid Avenue Yacht Club, Atlanta, Georgia, April 2006.

28. Travelers Club menu, also available at www.travelerstuba.com (accessed June 1, 2006).

29. James Mayse, "Model T On the Road to Recovery: Car Nearly Destroyed in Fire December 5 at Windy Hollow," *Messenger-Inquirer*, January 7, 2007.

30. Photos of the damage are at the Mackinac Bridgemen Museum website. www.mackinacbridgemenmuseum.com/gallery.php. This fire was also noted by Roadside America's Tourism News: "Mackinac Bridge Free Museum Burns Up." www.roadsideamerica.com/tnews/NewsItemDisplay.php?Tip_Attrid=%3D11083 (accessed December 26, 2007). See also John Walters, "Eagle Bridge Builder Keeps on Building," *Eagle Magazine*, Winter 1983. Reprinted on www.ironfest.com/jcs.html and "The Mackinaw Bridge Museum." www.ironfest.com/bridgemuseum.html (accessed December 26, 2007).

31. Isamu Takeda quoted in Bob Sylva, "Matchbook Memories: Each One in Isamu Takeda's Collection Has a Story to Tell," *Sacramento Bee*, April 1, 2007.

32. Frank McArdle quoted in Art Carey, "Tony Polito Keeps a Cut Above: Sharing the Buzz with an Old-School Barber," *The Philadelphia Inquirer*, April 28, 2007.

33. The Barber Pole Haircutting Parlors. www.thebarberpole.com (accessed June 5, 2007). See also photographer Rick Lee's photos of the Shear Cut on Fife Street, On Location with Rick Lee. rickleephoto.blogspot.com/search/label/barber (accessed June 6, 2007).

34. Label text, Ye Old Curiosity Shop, Seattle, Washington, January 2005.

35. Valueland, Lansing, Michigan, September 2004.

36. Scott Broden, "Street of Dreams: Blue Island's Olde Western Avenue Was Once a Bustling Place on Market Day. Now, After Harder Times, It's Seeing a Rebirth," *Chicago Tribune*, November 19, 1995.

37. Thomas Walsh, "Growth in Fernley Creates Demand for Casinos," *Reno Gazette-Journal*, May 10, 2004. www.rgj.com/news/stories.html (accessed 5 June 2007); Richard Moreno, "America's Loneliest Road Trip," *Nevada Magazine*. www.nevadamagazine.com/loneliess.roadtrip.html (accessed 5 June 2007); Christy Lattin, "Wigwam's Mary Royels Dies at Age 76," *Lahontan Valley News and Fallon Eagle Standard*, January 31, 2007. www.lahontanvalleynews.com/article/20070131/REGION/101310044 (accessed June 5, 2007).

38. Murphy's Bleachers. www.murphysbleachers.com (accessed June 22, 2006).

39. Nancy Moffett, "Jim Murphy, Owner of Bar Near Wrigley," *Chicago Sun-Times*, January 29, 2003. Costas Spirou and Larry Bennett name Murphy's Bleachers as one of the establishments representing Wrigleyville's gentrification. See *It's Hardly Sportin': Stadiums, Neighborhoods and the New Chicago* (DeKalb: Northern Illinois University Press, 2003), 138–139.

40. Lawrence A. Wenner, "In Search of the Sports Bar: Masculinity, Alcohol, Sports, and the Mediation of Public Space," in Genevieve Rail, ed., *Sport and Postmodern Times* (Albany: State University of New York Press, 1998), 301–332.

41. Dave Hoekstra, "Bernie's on Clark Serves Solace to Die Hard Cubs Fans," *Chicago Sun-Times*, September 7, 1990. Citysearch's comments on Rush Street can be found at chicago.citysearch.com/roundup/40097/ (accessed January 1, 2008).

42. Spirou and Bennett, *It's Hardly Sportin'*, 138.

43. Fran Spielman and Stephanie Zimmerman, "Wrigley Rooftop Tax Sought," *Chicago Sun-Times*, May 2, 1998.

44. Jim Murphy quoted in Richard A. Chapman, "White Sox-Cubs Rivalry Losing Some Meanness," *Chicago Sun-Times*, June 7, 1998. For figures on the Murphys' investment in the rooftop ordinance compliance, see Fran Spielman, "More Bleacher Seats, Night Games Likely to Get City OK," *Chicago Sun-Times*, June 19, 2001; Fran Spielman, "Wrigley Field Plan Won't Hurt Neighborhood View," *Chicago Sun-Times*, November 15, 2001; Teddy Greenstein, "Cubs Exec Battles on 2 Fronts: Mark McGuire is Directing Expansion Plans for Wrigley Field While Fighting Colon Cancer," *Chicago Tribune*, February 17, 2002.

45. Jim Murphy quoted in Crystal Yednak, "Wrigleyville Group Ends Owner's Bid to Raid Roof," *Chicago Tribune*, March 11, 2002. See also Lynette Kalsnes, "Beyond Bleachers, Folks See Pros, Cons," *Chicago Tribune*, June 19, 2001; Fran Spielman,

"Wrigley Field Plan Won't Hurt Neighborhood View: Tribune," *Chicago Sun-Times*, November 15, 2001.

46. Fran Spielman, "Foes of Wrigley Proposal Suggest Limited Expansion," *Chicago Tribune*, March 16, 2002; "Letters," *Chicago Sun-Times*, April 11, 2002; "Readers Sound Off On Rooftops," *Chicago Sun-Times*, April 14, 2002.

47. Rosalin Rossi and Fran Spielman, "Public Urination May Be Punished with a $500 Fine–'Our Neighborhood is Not a Washroom,'" Says Wrigley Alderman, *Chicago Sun-Times*, May 2, 2002; Will Potter and Bill Jauss, "Cubs Decry Expansion Denial: Neighbors' Fears Factor Into City's Rejection of Plans," *Chicago Tribune*, August 4, 2002.

48. Fran Spielman, "Daley Throws a Curve at Cubs–Mayor Says No New Night Games; Limits Ballpark Expansion," *Chicago Sun-Times*, August 4, 2002; Teddy Greenstein, "Cub Exec Battles on 2 Fronts," *Chicago Tribune*, February 17, 2002; Liam Ford and Rick Hepp, "Cubs Install Bleacher Screens–Groups Doubt Security Claim," *Chicago Tribune*, April 4, 2002.

49. Fran Spielman, "No New Cubs Night Games–Daley Throws Wrench in Trib's Plans," *Chicago Sun-Times*, August 3, 2002.

50. Gary Washburn, "Expansion Plans for Chicago's Wrigley Field Take a Big Hit," *Chicago Tribune*, December 14, 2002.

51. Fran Spielman, "Top This: Cubs Hit the Roofs With a Lawsuit," *Chicago Sun-Times*, December 17, 2002; Gary Washburn and Matt O'Connor, "Chicago Cubs Sue Neighborhood Rooftop Owners for Business Infringement," *Chicago Tribune*, December 17, 2002.

52. Brad Webber, "Jim Murphy, 54, Wrigleyville Bar Owner, Former Cop," *Chicago Tribune*, January 29, 2003. Nancy Moffett, "Jim Murphy, Owner of Bar Near Wrigley," *Chicago Sun-Times*, January 29, 2003.

53. Kurt Dewhurst and Marsha MacDowell, "Museum for the People: Museum Bars," *Material Culture* 18, no. 1 (Spring 1986): 37–49.

54. Office of Policy and Analysis, Smithsonian Institution, "Lure the Visitor: A Report for the National Museum of American History," (Washington, DC: Office of Policy and Analysis, July 2002). NMAH visitors were 86 percent white, while the Murphy's sample was 96 percent. Sixty-nine percent of NMAH visitors reported having either bachelor's or master's degrees, while 64 percent of the sample at Murphy's reported advanced degrees.

55. Visitor interview C4, Murphy's Bleachers, Chicago, Illinois, June 27, 2006.

56. Smithsonian, "Lure the Visitor," 16.

57. James Murphy, interview by author, Chicago, Illinois, June 27, 2006.

58. Visitor interviews C10 and C2, Murphy's Bleachers, Chicago, Illinois, June 27, 2006.

59. Visitor interview C12, Murphy's Bleachers, Chicago, Illinois, June 27, 2006. On the gentrification of Wrigleyville, see Costas Spirou and Larry Bennett, "Revamped Stadium . . . New Neighborhood?" *Urban Affairs Review* 37, no. 5 (May 2002): 675–702.

60. ZIP codes collected from respondents confirm this statement.

61. Alan Beardsworth and Alan Bryman, "Late Modernity and the Dynamics of Quasification," *The Sociological Review* 47, no. 2 (1999): 240.

CHAPTER SIX: LOCAL HISTORY, GLOBAL ECONOMY: THE FUNCTIONS OF HISTORY EXHIBITS IN THE SETTINGS OF EVERYDAY LIFE

1. Myron A. Marty, a history educator writing in 1978, summed up the educator debates in the twenty years preceding his essay. While the main point of contention was a single narrative versus inclusion of those traditionally left out of the grand narrative, the fundamental premise that history instruction produced a more responsible citizenry went unquestioned. Myron A. Marty, "National History in International Times," *The History Teacher* 12, no. 1 (November 1978), 45–55. Marguerite S. Shaffer examines nationalism and tourism in an earlier period. While most tourist activity focused on the natural environment, history was also thought to imbue citizens with a sense of national purpose. See Marguerite S. Shaffer, *See America First: Tourism and National Identity, 1880–1940* (Washington, DC: Smithsonian Institution Press, 2001), 193–202.

2. Tilden Rhea, *Race Pride and the American Identity* (Cambridge: Oxford University Press, 1997).

3. "The Art of Better Living," *Life*, September 25, 1944. UNCW Public History Teaching Collections. This ad is reproduced in Charles F. McGovern, *Sold American: Consumption and Citizenship, 1890–1930* (Chapel Hill: University of North Carolina Press, 2006), 357.

4. Lizabeth Cohen, *A Consumer's Republic: The Politics of Consumption in Postwar America* (New York: Vintage Books, 2004).

5. Marilyn Halter, *Shopping for Identity: The Marketing of Ethnicity* (New York: Schocken Books, 2000).

6. Halter, *Shopping for Identity*.

7. Ebron's study of tourists on a McDonald's-sponsored tour of Africa is one study that closely examines the relationship between consumerism and identity. Paulla Ebron, "Tourists as Pilgrims: Commercial Fashioning of Transatlantic Politics," *American Ethnologist* 26, no. 4: 910–32.

8. Juliet Schor, *The Overspent American: Upscaling, Downshifting, and the New Consumer* (New York: Basic Books, 1998); Juliet Schor, *The Overworked American: The Unexpected Decline of Leisure* (New York: Basic Books, 1991). For more on materialism in the United States in the 1980s, see Gil Troy, *Morning in America: How Ronald Reagan Invented the 1980s* (Princeton, NJ: Princeton University Press, 2005).

9. Ken Hillis, Michael Petit, Nathan Scott Epley, eds., in "Introducing Everyday eBay," *Everyday eBay: Culture, Collecting, and Desire* (New York: Routledge, 2006), 1.

10. Jennifer Harper, "Collectibles guide establishes the hierarchy of hip kitsch," *Washington Times*, January 1, 2001.

11. Russell Belk, *Collecting in a Consumer Society* (London and New York: Routledge, 1995), 87. Interestingly, this set of motivations provided the basis for an eBay marketing campaign, Shop Victoriously!, which featured people in highly competitive situations—like dog racing or fox hunting—in which the prize was a collector lunch box or vintage radio. For an overview, see Ann Christian-Diaz, "ebay: the auction site adds a new media play to its bag of marketing fun," *Creativity* (October 2007): 33.

12. Todd Gitlin, *Media Unlimited: How the Torrent of Images and Sounds Over-whelms Our Lives* (New York: Metropolitan, 2001), 17.

13. Mark Gottdiener, *The Theming of America: American Dreams, Media Fantasies, and Themed Environments* (Boulder, CO: Westview Press, 2001); B. Joseph Pine and James H. Gilmore, *The Experience Economy: Work is Theatre & Every Business a Stage* (Boston: Harvard Business School Press, 1999).

14. Bella Dicks, *Culture on Display: The Production of Contemporary Visitability* (Maidenhead, Berkshire, UK: Open University Press, 2003), 28.

15. Beverly Serrell, *Paying Attention: Visitors and Museum Exhibitions* (Washington, DC: American Association of Museums, 1998).

16. Gaea Leinhardt and Karen Knutson, *Listening In On Museum Conversations* (Walnut Creek, CA: AltaMira Press, 2004).

17. John Urry, "Mobility and Proximity," *Sociology* 36, no. 2 (May 2002): 264–65.

18. "Missouri's Little Museums: What They Lack in Size, They Make Up for in Charm," *St. Louis Post-Dispatch*, February 16, 1997.

19. "'Mr. Delta' Gave His All for Town and Museum," *The Denver Post*, July 9, 2006.

20. Lynne Iorio quoted in Myrna Petlicki, "Living in the Past: Lynne Iorio is Passionate About Park Ridge History," *Chicago Tribune*, November 22, 1998.

21. David Markiewicz, "Black Sports Shrine Just Needs Visitors," *Atlanta Journal-Constitution*, February 13, 2005.

22. Indy Teller quoted in Wendy Byerly Wood, "Carroll County Museums Opens in New Home," *The Mt. Airy News*, May 9, 2006. Teller's observation is true about the exhibits that provided field work for this study. During interviews, visitors often had difficulty relating how much time they had spent in the exhibit.

23. Visitor B5, interview by Author, Olde Mill House Printing Museum, June 9, 2006.

24. Amy Levin, "The Family Camping Hall of Fame and Other Wonders: Local Museums and Local Histories," *Studies in Popular Culture* 19, no. 3 (April 1997): 88.

25. Jennifer Eichstedt and Stephen Small, *Representations of Slavery: Race and Ideology in Southern Plantation Museums* (Washington, DC and London: Smithsonian Institution Press, 2002); James Loewen, *Lies Across America: What Our Historic Sites Get Wrong* (New York: Simon and Schuster, 1999).

26. Poudre Landmarks Foundation. poudrelandmarks.com/ (accessed July 3, 2007).

27. These examples are from responses to a needs assessment survey the author sent to small museums in 2006.

28. David Lowenthal, *The Heritage Crusade and the Spoils of History* (Cambridge: Cambridge University Press, 1998).

29. The "unusual museums" travel literature, while focusing on a particular type of small museum, is a good indicator of the appeal of smaller, less-professionalized museums. Michelle Lovric's recent addition to this literature covers small, specialized museums around the globe, sampling from Chile, Italy, England, Australia, The Netherlands, Belgium, Hungary, Spain, Greece, Japan, Malaysia, Poland, Switzerland, Iceland, the United States, and cyberspace. Michelle Lovric, *Cowgirls,*

Cockroaches and Celebrity Lingerie: The World's Most Unusual Museums (Thriplow, Cambridge, UK: Icon Books, 2007).

30. The US had 49.4 million arrivals in 2005, behind France's 76 million and Spain's 55.6 million. It leads the world in international tourism receipts at US$ 87 billion (followed by Spain's US$ 47.9 billion and France's US$ 42.3 billion). World Tourism Organization, "Facts and Figures," *Tourism Highlights 2006 Edition*. www. unwto.org (accessed June 28, 2007).

31. Visitor Survey TRR12, survey of international visitors to small U.S. museums, November 2007–September 2008.

32. Visitor Survey TRR05, international visitor survey.

33. This was a mail survey sent to two hundred small museums in the United States that focused on institutional features, visitation, and needs. Forty-two responded. The mailing list was compiled from "Historical Museum Guide to the United States." www.censusfinder.com/guide_to_historical_museums.htm (accessed September, 2006); Lynne Arany and Archie Hobson, *Little Museums: Over 1,000 Small and Not-so-Small American Showplaces* (New York: H. Holt, 1998); Lois Buttlar and Lubomyr Roman Wynar, *Guide to Information Resources in Ethnic Museum, Library, and Archival Collections in the United States* (Westport, CT: Greenwood Press, 1996).

34. Visitor SI66.

35. Visitor FF31.

36. Visitor B10, interview with author, Olde Mill House Printing Museum, Homosassa, Florida, June 9, 2006.

37. Jim DeCaire, interview with author, Ishpeming, Michigan, May 26, 2006.

38. Visitor C2, interview with author, Murphy's Bleachers, Chicago, Illinois, June 27, 2006.

39. See particularly Edward Bruner, *Culture on Tour: Ethnographies of Travel* (Chicago and London: University of Chicago Press, 2005); Yorke Rowan and Uzi Baram, *Marketing Heritage: Archaeology and the Consumption of the Past* (Walnut Creek, CA: AltaMira Press, 2004).

40. Dean MacCannell, *The Tourist: A New Theory of the Leisure Class* (Berkeley: University of California Press, 1989). See particularly chapter 5: "Staged Authenticity."

41. In addition to work by Bella Dicks, *Culture on Display*; and Barbara Kirshenblatt-Gimblett, *Destination Culture: Tourism, Museums, and Heritage* (Berkeley: University of California Press, 1998); see Michael Ames, *Cannibal Tours and Glass Boxes: The Anthropology of Museums* (Vancouver and Toronto: UBC Press, 1992); Steven C. Dubin, *Displays of Power: Controversy in the American Museum from the Enola Gay to Sensation* (New York: New York University Press, 1999); and Moira G. Simpson, *Making Representations: Museums in the Post-Colonial Era* (London and New York: Routledge, 1996).

42. Two significant exceptions to this are Christina Kreps, *Liberating Culture: Cross-Cultural Perspectives on Museums, Curation, and Heritage Preservation* (New York: Routledge, 2003), 46–78; and Nick Stanley, *Being Ourselves For You: The Global Display of Cultures* (London: Middlesex University Press, 1998).

43. Jim Anderson, interview with author, Homosassa, Florida, June 10, 2006.

44. Jack Barth, Doug Kirby, Ken Smith and Mike Wilkins, *Roadside America* (New York: Simon and Shuster, 1986); Doug Kirby, Ken Smith and Mike Wilkins, *The New Roadside America: The Modern Traveler's Guide to the Wild and Wonderful World of America's Tourist Attractions* (New York: Simon and Schuster, 1992), 112.

45. Wilkins, Smith, and Kirby, *The New Roadside America*, 117.

46. Joyce Jurnovoy and David Jenness, *America On Display: A Guide to Unusual Museums and Collections in the United States and Canada* (New York: Facts on File Publications, 1987), xviii–xix.

47. Mike Wilkins, Ken Smith, and Doug Kirby, "Your Online Guide to Offbeat Tourist Attractions." www.roadsideamerica.com/ (accessed May 30, 2008).

48. "Cotton Exchange History," The Cotton Exchange. www.shopcottonexchange.com/history.asp (accessed March 20, 2008).

49. "Cotton Exchange History."

50. The North Carolina Department of Commerce ranks New Hanover County's "travel impact" as 8th out of 100 counties in North Carolina. In 2006, tourism had a $388.31-million-dollar impact on the county, and its tourism growth had risen every year since 1991 with the exception of 2001, during which it saw a 2.91% decrease over the previous year. Wilmington is the largest city in the small county. North Carolina Department of Commerce. www.nccommerce.com/en/TourismServices/PromoteTravelAndTourismIndustry/TourismResearch/visitorspending.htm (accessed May 15, 2008).

51. Jerry Herron, *AfterCulture: Detroit and the Humiliation of History* (Detroit: Wayne State University Press, 1993). See also Robert Hollands and Paul Chatterton, "Producing Nightlife in the New Urban Entertainment Economy: Corporatization, Branding and Market Segmentation," *International Journal of Urban and Regional Research* 27, no. 2 (June 2003); and Mark Gottdiener, *The Theming of America: American Dreams, Media Fantasies, and Themed Environments* (Boulder, CO: Westview Press, 2001).

52. David Thelen, "Introduction," *History as Catalyst for Civic Dialogue: Case Studies from Animating Democracy* (Washington, DC: Americans for the Arts, 2005), vii.

53. Liz Sevcenko, Edgar W. Hopper, and Lisa Chice, "The Slave Galleries Restoration Project," *History as Catalyst for Civic Dialogue: Case Studies from Animating Democracy* (Washington, DC: Americans for the Arts, 2005), 25.

54. See particularly the works of James Loewen, *Lies Across America: What Our Historic Sites Get Wrong* (New York: Simon and Schuster, 1999) and *Lies My Teacher Told Me: Everything Your American History Textbook Got Wrong* (New York: Touchtone, 1996).

55. Ray Oldenburg, *The Great Good Place: Cafes, Coffee Shops, Bookstores, Bars, Hair Salons, and Other Hangouts at the Heart of a Community* (New York: Marlowe and Company, 1989, 1997, 1999), xxix.

56. Urry, "Mobility and Proximity," 265.

57. Loewen, *Lies Across America*, 25.

Bibliography

PRIMARY SOURCES

Museums and Other Sites of Historical Display

82nd Airborne Division War Memorial Museum, Fort Bragg, North Carolina
African American Heritage Museum of Wilmington, Wilmington, North Carolina
African American Sports Museum, Cobb County, Georgia
Alger County Heritage Center, Munising, Michigan
The American Sanitary Plumbing Museum, Worcester, Massachusetts
Androscoggin Historical Society Museum, Auburn, Maine
Anna Miller Museum and Red Onion Museum, Newcastle, Wyoming
Athens County Historical Society and Museum, Athens, Ohio
Avery House Museum, Fort Collins, Colorado
B&J's American Café, LaPorte, Indiana
The Barber Pole, New York, New York
Bellamy Mansion Museum of History and Design Arts, Wilmington, North Carolina
Bank of the Chickasaw Nation, Tishomingo, Oklahoma
Bennigan's Restaurant, various locations
Best Western McCoy's Inn and Conference Center, Ripley, West Virginia
Big Bear Valley Historical Museum, Big Bear City, California
Billy Sunday Visitors Center, Winona Lake, Indiana
Blackwell History of Education Museum, DeKalb, Illinois
Bladenboro Historical Society Museums, Bladenboro, North Carolina
Bruce Davis Home, Framingham, Massachusetts
Brunswick Town Historic Site, Winnabow, North Carolina
Camp Van Dorn World War II Museum, Centreville, Mississippi
Cape Fear Museum of History and Science, Wilmington, North Carolina

Casa Grande Valley Historical Society Museum, Casa Grande, Arizona
Champions Sports Bar, Washington, DC
The Charles H. Wright Museum of African American History, Detroit, Michigan
The Chicago Historical Society Museum, Chicago, Illinois
Chippewa County Historical Society Museum, Montevideo, Minnesota
City Reliquary, Brooklyn, New York
Claude Moore Colonial Farm, McLean, Virginia
Cokato Museum and Akerlund Photo Studio, Cokato, Minnesota
Columbus Historical Society Museum, Columbus, New Mexico
Columns-Pike County Historical Society Museum, Milford, Pennsylvania
Coos County Fairgrounds Museum, Myrtle Point, Oregon
Cordell Hull Birthplace State Park, Cookeville, Tennessee
The Cotton Exchange, Wilmington, North Carolina
Country Doctor Museum, Bailey, North Carolina
Cracker Barrel Restaurant, various locations
Czech Heritage Museum, Temple, Texas
Da Yoopers Tourist Trap and Museum, Ishpeming, Michigan
Delta County Historical Museum, Delta, Colorado
Edisto Island Museum, Edisto Island, South Carolina
Elton Tavern Museum, Burlington, California
Emil's Restaurant, Lansing, Michigan
Euclid Avenue Yacht Club, Atlanta, Georgia
Exotic World Burlesque Hall of Fame, Helendale, California
Fife Lake Historical Society Museum, Fife Lake, Michigan
First Baptist Church, Fairmont, North Carolina
First Due Fire Museum, Hazelwood, Missouri
Fort Fisher Historic Site, Kure Beach, North Carolina
The Freakatorium: El Museo Loco, New York, New York
Funeral Institute of Northeast Mortuary College, Norwood, Massachusetts
Garfield Farm Museum, Lafox, Illinois
Geary County Historical Society and Museum, Junction City, Kansas
The Grand Rapids Public Museum, Grand Rapids, Michigan
Ghost Walk of Old Wilmington, Wilmington, North Carolina
Glore Psychiatric Museum, St. Joseph, Missouri
Golden Drift Museum, Dutch Flat, California
Great Harbor Maritime Museum, Northeast Harbor, Maine
Great Plains Welsh Heritage Center, Wymore, Nebraska
Hard Rock Café, London
Hebrew Union Temple, Greenville, Mississippi
Holy United Methodist Church, Houston, Texas
Hope Historical Museum, Hope, New Jersey
Homewood Historical Society Museum, Homewood, Illinois
Ilanka Cultural Center and Museum, Cordova, Alaska
Independence Bank, Owensboro, Kentucky
International Museum of Surgical Science, Chicago, Illinois
Ivar's Acres of Clams, Seattle, Washington
IXL Museum, Hermansville, Michigan

Jebens Hardware Store, Chicago, Illinois
JFK Special Warfare Museum, Fort Bragg, North Carolina
Kell House Museum, Wichita Falls, Texas
Knott's Berry Farm, Buena Park, California
Lanai Barber Shop, Sacramento, California
LaPorte Historical Society Museum, LaPorte, Indiana
Lone Jack Civil War Museum, Lone Jack, Missouri
The Levi Strauss and Company Museum, San Francisco, California
Liberty Antiques Mall, Dewitt, Michigan
Lyon County Historical Society Museum, Emporia, Kansas
Mackinac Bridge Museum in Mama Mia's Pizza, Mackinac City, Michigan
Mary and Moe's Wigwam, Fernley, Nevada
McAllister House Museum, Colorado Springs, Colorado
McDonald's Restaurant, various locations
McHenry County Historical Society Museum, Union, Illinois
The Middlefield Cheese Factory Museum, Middlefield, Ohio
Moores Creek National Battlefield, Currie, North Carolina
Mount Tabor School, Tabor City, North Carolina
Murphy's Bleachers, Chicago, Illinois
Museum of Coastal Carolina, Ocean Isle Beach, North Carolina
National Fred Harvey Museum, Leavenworth, Kansas
New Orleans Historic Voodoo Museum, New Orleans, Louisiana
Old Baldy Foundation and Smith Island Museum of History, Bald Head Island, North Carolina
The Olde Mill House Printing Museum, Old Homosassa, Florida
Packwood House Museum, Lewisburg, Pennsylvania
The Palace of the Governors, Santa Fe, New Mexico
Park Ridge Historical Society Museum, Park Ridge, Illinois
Penderlea Homestead Museum, Willard, North Carolina
Pioneer Farm Museum, Eatonville, Washington
Pullman Porters Museum, Chicago, Illinois
River Road African American Museum, Donaldsonville, Louisiana
Rock and Roll and Blues Heritage Museum, Clarksdale, Mississippi
Rocky Mount Historical Association Museum, Piney Flats, Tennessee
Sanders Courts, Corbin, Kentucky
Schmidt House Museum, Grants Pass, Oregon
Second Church, Newton, Massachusetts
Shear Cut on Fife Street, Charleston, West Virginia
Shore Line Trolley Museum, East Haven, Connecticut
Shoshone-Bannock Tribal Museum, Fort Hall, Idaho
Sod House Museum, Aline, Oklahoma
SPJST Library, Archives, and Museum, Temple, Texas
Texas Pharmacy Museum, Amarillo, Texas
Tony Polito's Barber Shop and Military Museum, West Chester, Pennsylvania
Traveler's Club and Tuba Museum, Okemos, Michigan
National Border Patrol Museum, El Paso, Texas
Negaunee Historical Museum, Negaunee, Michigan

The Unknown Museum, Mill Valley, California
Upper Peninsula Sports Hall of Fame, Famer's Bar, Iron Mountain, Michigan
Valueland, Lansing, Michigan
Vermillion County Museum, Danville, Illinois
Victoria Station, San Francisco
Washington County Farm Museum, Greenwich, New York
The Wells Fargo Museum, multiple locations
Windy Hollow Restaurant and Museum, Owensboro, Kentucky
The World of Coca-Cola, Atlanta, Georgia
Wyoming Frontier Prison, Rawlins, Wyoming
Ye Olde Curiosity Shop, Seattle, Washington

Surveys and Interviews

Videorecorded Interviews

Anderson, James, Olde Mill House Printing Museum, Old Homosassa, Florida
DeCaire, Jim, Da Yoopers Tourist Trap and Museum, Ishpeming, Michigan
Devinney, Rosemary, Shoshone-Bannock Tribal Museum, Fort Hall, Idaho
Eschief, April, Shoshone-Bannock Tribal Museum, Fort Hall, Idaho
Farmer, Delbert, Shoshone-Bannock Tribal Museum, Fort Hall, Idaho
Houtz, Rusty, Shoshone-Bannock Tribal Museum, Fort Hall, Idaho
Murphy, James, Murphy's Bleachers, Chicago, Illinois

Interviews

Exit interviews with 89 visitor groups at:
Shoshone-Bannock Tribal Museum
Olde Mill House Printing Museum
Da Yoopers Tourist Trap and Museum
Murphy's Bleachers
Needs Assessment Survey of Small Museums, 2006 (41 total responses)
Survey of International Visitors to Small Museums, 2007-2008 (70 total responses)

Web Sites and Blogs

The Barber Pole Haircutting Parlors, www.thebarberpole.com
City-Data.com, www.city-data.com/zips/49847.html
Dragonfly Enterprises, www.drgnfly4g.com/
First Due Fire Museum, www.firstduefiremuseum.com/services.html
Florida Secrets, www.floridasecrets.com/Restaurants/WC/MuseumCafe.htm
The Freakatorium: El Museo Loco, www.freakatorium.com/events.html
GoNomad, http://www.gonomad.com/
Leonard's Public Gallery, picasaweb.google.com/Leonardgrill
Hebrew Union Congregation, www.hebrewunion.org/

Historical Museum Guide to the United States, www.censusfinder.com/guide_to_ historical_museums.htm

The History Factory, www.historyfactory.com/index.aspx?sectionid=23

HistoryLink.org: The Online Encyclopedia of Washington State University, historylink.org

Hyphen: Asian America Unabridged, www.hyphenmagazine.com/

IgoUgo, www.igougo.com/

Mackinac Bridgemen Museum, www.mackinacbridgemenmuseum.com/gallery.php

Murphy's Bleachers, www.murphysbleachers.com

Penderlea Homestead Museum, www.penderleahomesteadmuseum.org/

Rick Lee Photo, rickleephoto.blogspot.com/search/label/barber

Roadside America, roadsideamerica.com

Sound Partners for Community Health, www.soundpartners.org/node/1672

Traveler's Club and Tuba Museum, www.travelerstuba.com

Washington County Fair, www.washingtoncountyfair.com/museum.htm

World of Coca-Cola, www.woccatlanta.com

Travel Guides and Exhibition Catalogues

Arany, Lynne, and Archie Hobson. *Little Museums: Over 1,000 Small and Not-so-Small American Showplaces.* New York: H. Holt, 1998.

Buttlar, Lois, and Lubomyr Roman Wynar. *Guide to Information Resources in Ethnic Museum, Library, and Archival Collections in the United States.* Westport, CT: Greenwood Press, 1996.

The Dead Sea Scrolls: Catalog of the Exhibition of Scrolls and Artifacts from the Collections of the Israel Antiquities Authority. Grand Rapids, MI: Public Museum of Grand Rapids, 2003. www.grmuseum.org/exhibits/dead_sea_scrolls/images/navigation/ exhibition.shtml (accessed January 20, 2006).

Des Garennes, Christine. *Great Little Museums of the Midwest.* Black Earth, WI: Trails Books, 2002.

Jurnovoy, Joyce, and David Jenness. *America On Display: A Guide to Unusual Museums and Collections in the United States and Canada.* New York: Facts on File Publications, 1987.

Kirby, Doug, Ken Smith and Mike Wilkins. *The New Roadside America: The Modern Traveler's Guide to the Wild and Wonderful World of America's Tourist Attractions.* New York: Simon and Schuster, 1992.

Rubin, Saul. *Offbeat Museums: The Collections and Curators of America's Most Unusual Museums.* Santa Monica, CA: Santa Monica Press, 1997.

Newspapers and Magazines

Amarillo Globe-News, Amarillo, Texas

Atlanta Journal-Constitution, Atlanta, Georgia

The Boston Globe, Boston, Massachusetts

The Charlotte Observer, Charlotte, North Carolina

Chicago Sun-Times, Chicago, Illinois

The Chicago Tribune, Chicago, Illinois
Creativity, Toronto, Ontario
The Daily Reflector, Greenville, North Carolina
The Denver Post, Denver, Colorado
The Fayetteville Observer, Fayetteville, North Carolina
Messenger-Inquirer, Owensboro, Kentucky
The Houston Chronicle, Houston, Texas
Lahontan Valley News and Fallon Eagle Standard, Fallon, Nevada
The Lay of the Land: The Center for Land Use Interpretation Newsletter, Culver City, California
Life Magazine, New York, New York
Mackinac Bridge Museum in Mama Mia's Pizza, Mackinac City, Michigan
Marin Independent Journal, Novato, California
Nevada Magazine, Carson City, Nevada
New York Times Magazine, New York, New York
The News and Observer, Raleigh, North Carolina
The Philadelphia Inquirer, Philadelphia, Pennsylvania
Reading Eagle, Reading, Pennsylvania
Reno Gazette-Journal, Reno, Nevada
Richmond Times-Dispatch, Richmond, Virginia
Sacramento Bee, Sacramento, California
San Francisco Chronicle, San Francisco, California
The Seattle Times, Seattle, Washington
Sports Illustrated, Los Angeles, California
St. Louis Post Dispatch, Saint Louis, Missouri
Washington Post, Washington, DC
The Washington Times, Washington, DC
Museum News, American Association of Museums, Washington, DC

SECONDARY SOURCES

Ames, Kenneth, Barbara Franco, and L. Thomas Frye, eds., *Ideas and Images: Developing Interpretive History Exhibits.* Walnut Creek, CA: Alta Mira Press, 1997.

Ames, Michael. *Cannibal Tours and Glass Boxes: The Anthropology of Museums.* Vancouver and Toronto: UBC Press, 1992.

Archibald, Robert R. *The New Town Square: Museums and Communities in Transition.* Walnut Creek, CA: AltaMira Press, 2004.

Barth, Jack, Doug Kirby, Ken Smith and Mike Wilkins. *Roadside America.* New York; Simon and Shuster, 1986.

Bean, Jonathan J. *Beyond the Broker State: Federal Policies Toward Small Business, 1936–1961.* Chapel Hill and London: The University of North Carolina Press, 1996.

Beardsworth, Alan, and Alan Bryman. "Late Modernity and the Dynamics of Quasification." *The Sociological Review* 47, no. 2 (1999): 228–57.

Belk, Russell. *Collecting in a Consumer Society.* London and New York: Routledge, 1995.

Bennett, Tony. *The Birth of the Museum: History, Theory, Politics.* New York: Routledge, 1995.

Blackford, Mansel G. *A History of Small Business in America,* 2nd ed. Chapel Hill and London: University of North Carolina Press, 2003.

Blom, Thomas. "Morbid Tourism: A Postmodern Market Niche with an Example from Althorp." *Norwegian Journal of Geography* 54, no. 1 (2001): 29–36.

Blumin, Stuart. *The Emergence of the Middle Class: Social Experience in the American City, 1760–1900.* Cambridge: Cambridge University Press, 1989.

Bruner, Edward. *Culture on Tour: Ethnographies of Travel.* Chicago and London: University of Chicago Press, 2005.

Christian-Diaz, Ann. "ebay: the auction site adds a new media play to its bag of marketing fun." *Creativity* (October 2007): 33.

Cohen, Lizabeth. *A Consumer's Republic: The Politics of Consumption in Postwar America.* New York: Vintage Books, 2004.

Danilov, Victor. *Corporate Museums, Galleries, and Visitor Centers: A Directory.* Westport, CT: Greenwood Press, 1991.

——. *A Planning Guide for Corporate Museums, Galleries, and Visitor Centers.* New York: Greenwood Press, 1992.

Dennet, Andrea, and Stulman Dennett. *Weird and Wonderful: The Dime Museum in America.* New York and London: New York University Press, 1997.

Deutsch, Jennifer. *Just Who Do Your Customers Think You Are?: A Guide to Branding Your Organization.* Lansing, MI: Michigan Museums Association, 2002.

Dewhurst, Kurt, and Marsha MacDowell, "Museum for the People: Museum Bars." *Material Culture* 18, no. 1 (Spring 1986): 37–49.

Diamond, Judy. *Practical Evaluation Guide: Tools for Museums and Other Informal Educational Settings.* Lanham, MD: AltaMira Press, 1999.

Dicks, Bella. *Culture on Display: The Production of Contemporary Visitability.* Maidenhead, Berkshire, UK: Open University Press, 2003.

Dougherty, Ryan. "Haunting History." *National Parks* 77, no. 9 (September 2003).

Dubin, Steven C. *Displays of Power: Controversy in the American Museum from the Enola Gay to Sensation.* New York: New York University Press, 1999.

Ebron, Paulla. "Tourists as Pilgrims: Commercial Fashioning of Transatlantic Politics." *American Ethnologist* 26, no. 4: 910–32.

Eichstedt, Jennifer, and Stephen Small. *Representations of Slavery: Race and Ideology in Southern Plantation Museums.* Washington, DC and London: Smithsonian Institution Press, 2002.

Fliotsos, Anne. "Gotta Get a Gimmick: The Burlesque Career of Millie De Leon." *Journal of American Culture* 21, no. 4 (Winter 1998): 1–8.

Florida, Richard. *The Rise of the Creative Class and How It's Transforming Work, Leisure, Community and Everyday Life.* New York: Basic Books, 2000.

Friedman, Ted. "The World of *The World of Coca-Cola*." *Communication Research* 19, no. 5 (October 1992): 642–62.

Frisch, Michael. *A Shared Authority: Essays on the Craft and Meaning of Oral and Public History.* Albany, NY: State University of New York Press, 1990.

Gere, Charlie. *Digital Culture.* London: Reaktion Books, 2002.

Gilmore, James H. *The Experience Economy: Work is Theatre & Every Business a Stage.* Boston, MA: Harvard Business School Press, 1999.

Gitlin, Todd. *Media Unlimited: How the Torrent of Images and Sounds Overwhelms Our Lives*. New York: Metropolitan Books, 2001.

Gordon, Tammy S. "Palace of the Governors." *The Public Historian* 29, no. 4 (Fall 2007): 91–93.

Gottdiener, Mark. *The Theming of America: American Dreams, Media Fantasies, and Themed Environments*. Boulder, CO: Westview Press, 2001.

Halter, Marilyn. *Shopping for Identity: The Marketing of Ethnicity*. New York: Schocken Books, 2000.

Handler, Richard, and Eric Gable. *The New History in an Old Museum: Creating the Past at Colonial Williamsburg*. Durham and London: Duke University Press, 1997.

Haraway, Donna. "Situated Knowledges: The Science Question in Feminism and the Privilege of Partial Perspective." *Feminist Studies* 3 (Fall 1988): 575–99.

Harden, Victoria. "Museum Exhibit Standards: Do Historians Really Want Them?" *The Public Historian* 21, no. 3 (Summer 1999): 91–109.

Harris, Neil. "The World of Coca-Cola." *The Journal of American History* 82, no. 1 (June 1995): 154–58.

Hein, George. *Learning in the Museum*. New York: Routledge, 1998.

Herron, Jerry. *AfterCulture: Detroit and the Humiliation of History*. Detroit: Wayne State University Press, 1993.

Hillis, Ken, Michael Petit, and Nathan Scott Epley, eds. *Everyday eBay: Culture, Collecting, and Desire*. New York: Routledge, 2006.

Hollands, Robert, and Paul Chatterton. "Producing Nightlife in the New Urban Entertainment Economy: Corporatization, Branding and Market Segmentation." *International Journal of Urban and Regional Research* 27, no. 2 (June 2003): 361–85.

Hooper-Greenhill, Eilean. *Museums and the Interpretation of Visual Culture*. New York: Routledge, 2000.

Hudson, Kenneth. *A Social History of Museums: What the Visitors Thought*. Atlantic Highlands, NJ: Humanities Press, 1975.

Jaher, Frederic Cople, ed. *The Age of Industrialism in America: Essays in Social Structure and Cultural Values*. New York: The Free Press, 1968.

Jakle, John A., and Keith A. Sculle. *Fast Food: Roadside Restaurants in the Automobile Age*. Baltimore and London: The Johns Hopkins University Press, 1999.

Johnson, G. Wesley. "The Origins of the Public Historian and the National Council on Public History." *The Public Historian* 21, no. 3 (Summer 1999): 167–80.

Kammen, Carol. *On Doing Local History*, 2nd ed. Walnut Creek, CA: AltaMira Press, 2003.

Kammen, Michael. *Mystic Chords of Memory: The Transformation of Tradition in American Culture*. New York: Knopf, 1991.

Karp, Ivan, Christine Mullen Kreamer, and Steven D. Lavine. *Museums and Communities: The Politics of Public Culture*. Washington, DC and London: Smithsonian Institution Press, 1992.

Kempers, Margot. *Community Matters: An Exploration of Theory and Practice*. Chicago: Burnham Publishers, 2002.

Kirby, Doug, Ken Smith and Mike Wilkins. *The New Roadside America: The Modern Traveler's Guide to the Wild and Wonderful World of America's Tourist Attractions*. New York: Simon and Schuster, 1992.

Kirshenblatt-Gimblett, Barbara. *Destination Culture: Tourism, Museums, and Heritage*. Berkeley: University of California Press, 1998.

Korza, Pam, and Barbara Schaffer Bacon, eds. *History as Catalyst for Civic Dialogue: Case Studies from Animating Democracy*. Washington, DC: Americans for the Arts, 2005.

Kreps, Christina. *Liberating Culture: Cross-Cultural Perspectives on Museums, Curation, and Heritage Preservation*. New York: Routledge, 2003.

Lamont, Michele. *The Dignity of Working Men: Morality and the Boundaries of Race, Class and Immigration*. Cambridge: Harvard University Press, 2000.

Leinhardt, Gaea, and Karen Knutson. *Listening In on Museum Conversations*. Walnut Creek, CA: AltaMira Press, 2004.

Levin, Amy. "The Family *Camping* Hall of Fame and Other Wonders: Local Museums and Local Histories." *Studies in Popular Culture* 19, no. 3 (April 1997): 77–90.

Levin, Amy, ed. *Defining Memory: Local Museums and the Construction of History in America's Changing Communities*. Lanham, MD: AltaMira Press, 2007.

Levenstein, Harvey. *Paradox of Plenty: A Social History of Eating in Modern America*. New York: Oxford University Press, 1993.

Loewen, James. *Lies Across America: What Our Historic Sites Get Wrong*. New York: Simon and Schuster, 1999.

Loewen, James. Lies My Teacher Told Me: *Everything Your American History Textbook Got Wrong*. New York: Touchtone, 1996.

Lovric, Michelle. *Cowgirls, Cockroaches and Celebrity Lingerie: The World's Most Unusual Museums*. Thriplow, Cambridge, UK: Icon Books, 2007).

Lowenthal, David. *The Heritage Crusade and the Spoils of History*. Cambridge: Cambridge University Press, 1998.

Luxenberg, Stan. *Roadside Empires: How the Chains Franchised America*. New York: Viking Penguin, 1985.

MacCannell, Dean. *The Tourist: A New Theory of the Leisure Class*. Berkeley: University of California Press, 1989.

Marty, Myron A. "National History in International Times." *The History Teacher* 12, no. 1 (November 1978): 45–55.

McGovern, Charles F. *Sold American: Consumption and Citizenship, 1890–1930*. Chapel Hill: University of North Carolina Press, 2006.

McLean, Kathleen. *Planning for People in Museum Exhibitions*. Washington, DC: Association of Science-Technology Centers, 1993.

Mead, Sidney Moko. "Indigenous Models of Museums in Oceania." *Museum* 35, no. 139 (1983): 98–101.

Meringolo, Denise. "Capturing the Public Imagination: The Social and Professional Place of Public History." *American Studies International* 42, nos. 2 & 3 (June–October 2004): 86–117.

Miller, Marla R. "Playing to Strength: Teaching Public History at the Turn of the 21st Century." *American Studies International* 42, nos. 2 & 3 (June–October 2004): 174–212.

Newell, Jay. "Revisiting Schramm's Radiotown: Media Displacement and Saturation." *Journal of Radio Studies* 14, no. 1: 3–19.

Novick, Peter. *That Noble Dream: The "Objectivity Question" and the American Historical Profession*. Cambridge: Cambridge University Press, 1988.

Office of Policy and Analysis, Smithsonian Institution. "Lure the Visitor: A Report for the National Museum of American History." Washington, DC: Office of Policy and Analysis, July 2002.

Oldenburg, Ray. *The Great Good Place: Cafes, Coffee Shops, Bookstores, Bars, Hair Salons and Other Hangouts at the Heart of a Community.* New York: Marlowe and Company, 1989, 1997, 1999.

Pekarik, Andrew. "Engineering Answers." *Curator: The Museum Journal* 47, no. 2: 145–48.

Pillsbury, Richard. *No Foreign Food: The American Diet in Time and Place.* Boulder, CO: Westview Press, 1998.

Pine, B. Joseph and James H. Gilmore. *The Experience Economy: Work is Theatre & Every Business a Stage.* Boston: Harvard Business School Press, 1999.

Piore, Michael. "The Reconfiguration of Work and Employment Relations in the United States at the Turn of the Century." *Advances in Life Course Research* 8: 23–44.

Poster, Mark. *Information Please: Culture and Politics in the Age of Digital Machines.* Durham and London: Duke University Press, 2006.

Prown, Jules David. "The Truth of Material Culture: History or Fiction?" in Prown and Kenneth Haltman, *American Artifacts: Essays in Material Culture.* East Lansing: Michigan State University Press, 2000.

Rabinovitz, Lauren, and Abraham Geil, eds. *Memory Bytes: History, Technology, and Digital Culture.* Durham and London: Duke University Press, 2004.

Rectanus, Mark. *Culture Incorporated: Museums, Artists, and Corporate Sponsorships.* Minneapolis: University of Minnesota Press, 2002.

Rosenzweig, Roy, and David Thelen. *The Presence of the Past: Popular Uses of History in American Life.* New York: Columbia University Press, 1998.

Rowan, Yorke, and Uzi Baram. *Marketing Heritage: Archaeology and the Consumption of the Past.* Walnut Creek, CA: AltaMira Press, 2004.

Rhea, Tilden. *Race Pride and the American Identity.* Cambridge: Harvard University Press, 1997.

Russo, David J. *Keepers of Our Past: Local Historical Writing in the United States, 1820s–1930s.* New York: Greenwood Press, 1988.

Sandell, Richard, ed. *Museums, Society, Inequality.* London and New York: Routledge, 2002.

Sevcenko, Liz, Edgar W. Hopper, and Lisa Chice. "The Slave Galleries Restoration Project." *History as Catalyst for Civic Dialogue: Case Studies from Animating Democracy.* Washington, DC: Americans for the Arts, 2005.

Shactman, Tom. *Around the Block: The Business of a Neighborhood.* New York: Harcourt Brace, 1997.

Shaffer, Marguerite S. *See America First: Tourism and National Identity, 1880–1940.* Washington, DC: Smithsonian Institution Press, 2001.

Schoem, David, and Sylvia Hurtado. *Intergroup Dialogue: Deliberative Democracy in School, College, Community, and Workplace.* Ann Arbor: University of Michigan Press, 2001.

Schor, Juliet. *The Overspent American: Upscaling, Downshifting, and the New Consumer.* New York: Basic Books, 1998.

———. *The Overworked American: The Unexpected Decline of Leisure.* New York: Basic Books, 1991.

Schulz, Constance B. "An Academic Balancing Act: Public History Education Today." *The Public Historian* 21, no. 3 (Summer 1999): 143–54.

Serrell, Beverly. *Paying Attention: Visitors and Museum Exhibitions.* Washington, DC: American Association of Museums, 1998.

Serrell, Beverly. *Exhibit Labels: An Interpretive Approach.* Walnut Creek, CA: AltaMira Press, 1996.

Sherry, John. "Media Saturation and Entertainment-Education," *Communication Theory* 12, no. 2 (May 2002): 206–24.

Simpson, Moira G. *Making Representations: Museums in the Post-Colonial Era.* London and New York: Routledge, 1996.

Spirou, Costas, and Larry Bennett. *It's Hardly Sportin': Stadiums, Neighborhoods and the New Chicago.* DeKalb: Northern Illinois University Press, 2003.

———. "Revamped Stadium . . . New Neighborhood?" *Urban Affairs Review* 37, no. 5 (May 2002): 675–702.

Stanley, Nick. *Being Ourselves for You: The Global Display of Cultures.* London: Middlesex University Press, 1998.

Starn, Randolph. "A Historian's Brief Guide to New Museum Studies." *American Historical Review* 110, no. 1 (February 2005): 68–98.

Stowe, Steven. *Doctoring the South: Southern Physicians and Everyday Medicine in the Mid-Nineteenth Century.* Chapel Hill: University of North Carolina Press, 2004.

Thelen, David. "Introduction," *History as Catalyst for Civic Dialogue: Case Studies from Animating Democracy.* Washington, DC: Americans for the Arts, 2005.

Troy, Gil. *Morning in America: How Ronald Reagan Invented the 1980s.* Princeton, NJ: Princeton University Press, 2005.

Ulrich, Laurel Thatcher. *The Age of Homespun: Objects and Stories in the Creation of an American Myth.* New York: Vintage Books, 2001.

Urry, John. "Mobility and Proximity." *Sociology* 36, no. 2 (May 2002): 264–65.

———. *The Tourist Gaze: Leisure and Travel in Contemporary Societies.* London: Sage Publications, 1990.

Wallace, Margot A. *Museum Branding: How to Create and Maintain Image, Loyalty, and Support.* Lanham, MD: AltaMira Press, 2006.

Wallace, Mike. *Mickey Mouse History and Other Essays on American Memory.* Philadelphia: Temple University Press, 1996.

Welch, Deborah. "Teaching Public History: Strategies for Undergraduate Program Development." *The Public Historian* 25, no. 1 (Winter 2003): 71–82.

Wenner, Lawrence A. "In Search of the Sports Bar: Masculinity, Alcohol, Sports, and the Mediation of Public Space," in Genevieve Rail, ed., *Sport and Postmodern Times.* Albany: State University of New York Press, 1998: 301–32.

West, Patricia. *Domesticating History: The Political Origins of America's House Museums.* Washington, DC: Smithsonian Institution Press, 1999.

Wheeler, Leigh Ann. "Battling Over Burlesque: Conflicts Between Maternalism, Paternalism, and Organized Labor, 1920–1932." *Frontiers: A Journal of Women Studies* 20, no. 2 (1999): 148–74.

Wilentz, Sean. *Chants Democratic: New York City and the Rise of the American Working Class, 1788–1850.* New York and Oxford: Oxford University Press, 1984.

Index

82nd Airborne Division War Memorial
Museum, 65

academic exhibition. *See* exhibits
African American history, 16, 20–21,
25, 45–46, 71–74
African-American Sports Museum, 104
Alamo, 98
Alger County Historical Society
Heritage Center, 44–45
American Association for State and
Local History (AASLH), 38
American Association of Museums,
20
American Historical Association (AHA),
37–38
American Sanitary Plumbing Museum,
26
Anderson, Jim, 24–25, 71–74, 109
Animating Democracy, 112–113
The Antiques Roadshow, 101
Anzuoni, Bob, 65
artifact preservation, 84
artisans, 60, 67
Atlanta Fishing Club, 74
authority, 30
Avery House Museum, 105

B&J's American Café, 27–28, 84
The Barber Pole, 85
barber shops, 85
Belk, Russell, 102
Bennett, Tony, 10
Bennigan's, 77
Best Western McCoy's Inn and
Conference Center, 85
Beth Ahabah Museum and Archives, 47
Billy Sunday Home and Visitors Center,
49–51
Blackwell History of Education
Museum, 61
Bulmann, Art, 86

Cabela's, 102
Champions, 78–79. *See also* sports bars
Chicago History Museum, 19–20
Claude Moore Colonial Farm, 67
Columbus Historical Society Museum,
40
community exhibition. *See* exhibits
The Confederama, 110
consumerism, 97, 101–102
corporate exhibition. *See* exhibits
corporatism, 60
Cottle, Ann, 34

The Cotton Exchange, 110–112
Country Doctor Museum, 62–63
Cracker Barrel, 77

Danilov, Victor, 21
Dasbach, Theo, 106
Davis, Bruce, 50
DeCaire, Jim, 67, 108
Delta County Historical Society
    Museum, 40, 104
Devinney, Rosemary, 41–42, 44, 109
Dewhurst, Kurt, 26, 93
Dicks, Bella, 10
digital communication, 6, 70, 74,
    102

eBay, 101
economy: global, 5, 12, 74, 97, 102;
    leisure, 6, 12, 78–80, 91, 95; and
    small business, 60
Egdorf, Elain, 40
Elliot, Marilyn, 40
Emil's, 80
entrepreneurial exhibition. *See* exhibits
Eschief, April, *41*
ethnic identity, 98
Euclid Avenue Yacht Club, 29, 82–83
Evans, Dixie, 8, 62
exhibits: academic, 11, 16–21, *17–18*;
    community, 11–13, *17–18*, 22–24,
    31, 35–52, 97; corporate, 11,
    17–18, 21–22; entrepreneurial,
    11–13, *17–18*, 24–26, 31, 59–74,
    97; epistemology of, 7, 36, 42,
    52, 104; in bars, 78–85, 89–93; in
    churches, 46; in farm museums,
    66–67; in large museums, 4; in non-
    museum settings, 4, 77–93; in small
    museums, 4, 38–39; in temples,
    46; in thrift stores, 86, *88*; types of,
    10–11; vernacular, 11–13, *17–18*,
    26–29, 31, 75–93, 97

Famer's Bar and Upper Peninsula
    Sports Hall of Fame, *81*
farm museums, 66–67
Farmer, Delbert, 42, 44

Fife Lake Area Historical Museum, *55*
Fike, Nancy, 49
First Due Fire Museum, 59
Fort Fisher State Historic Site, 107
Fox, Johnny, 62
Freakatorium: El Museo Loco, 62
Frisch, Michael, 9
Funeral Institute of Northeast Mortuary
    College, 61

Gere, Charlie, 70
ghost tours, 47, 49
Glore, George, 64
Glore Psychiatric Museum, *64–65*
Grand Rapids Public Museum, 16
Great Plains Welsh Heritage Museum,
    54
Greektown, 77
guidebooks, 27, 106, 109–110

Hambrick, Kathe, 46
Hard Rock Café, 78, 102
Harraway, Donna, 8
Hebrew Union Congregation, 23,
    46–47
Herron, Jerry, 77
Hodgin, Gordon, 40, 104
Homewood Historical Society, 40
Houtz, Rusty, 42–44

Immigration and Nationality Act of
    1965, 99
indigenous curation, 9, 22–23, 36
International Museum of Surgical
    Science, 63
Iorio, Lynne, 104
Ivar's Acres of Clams, 75–76
IXL Museum, 54, 56–57

Jebens Hardware Store, 86
JFK Special Warfare Museum, 65–66
Johnson, G. Wesley, 8

Kammen, Carol, 39
Kentucky Nurses Association, 61–62
Knott's Berry Farm, 78
Kreps, Christina, 36

Lamont, Michele, 60
Lanai Barber Shop, 85
LaPorte Historical Society Museum, *23*,
    47–48
Levi Strauss & Company Museum, 21
Levin, Amy, 36, 104–105
Liberty Antiques Mall, 28–29
Little Bighorn National Battlefield, 98
Little League World Series Museum,
    108
Lone Jack Civil War Museum, 104

MacDowell, Marsha, 93
Mackinac Bridge Museum, 84
Manoog, Charles, 26
Manzanar, 98
market segmentation, 13, 98–101
Martin Luther King, Jr. Birthplace, 98
Mary and Moe's Wigwam, 89
McCannell, Dean, 108
McDonald's, 77
McGowan, Mickey, 50–51
McHenry County Historical Society
    Museum, 49
McLean, Kathleen, 7
Mead, Sidney Moko, 36
Meringolo, Denise, 38
Merritt, Roxanne, 65
Middlefield Cheese Factory Museum,
    25–26
military museums, 65
Murphy, Jr., James, 84, 95
Murphy, Jim, 89–93
Murphy's Bleachers, 12, 26, 89–96, 108
museum studies, 9

National Baseball Hall of Fame and
    Museum, 108
National Border Patrol Museum, 66
National Museum of American History
    (NMAH), 94
Negro Leagues Baseball Museum, 108
New Orleans Historic Voodoo
    Museum, 105

O'Harro, Mike, 78–79
Ye Olde Curiosity Shoppe, 7, 85–87

Olde Mill House Printing Museum,
    24–25, 70–74, 104, 107, 109
Oldenburg, Ray, 114

Palace of the Governors, 20
Pappas, Billie and John, 27
Penderlea Homestead Museum, 33–*34*,
    35
Pioneer Farm Museum, 67
professions, 61
Prown, Jules, 7
public history scholarship, 8

Rectanus, Mark, 21
Rhea, Tilden, 98
River Road African American Museum,
    46
Rock n Roll and Blues Heritage
    Museum, 105–106
Rosenzweig, Roy, 5, 31, 38, 49
Russo, David, 37

Sanders Courts, 78
Schor, Juliet, 101
Shoshone Bannock Tribal Museum, 11,
    40–44, 46, 53–54, 56, 103, 109
Small Business Administration, 60
Smith Island Museum, 107
Spainhour, Irene, 104
sports bars, 78–85, 89–93
Stanley, Nick, 9, 22, 36, 52
Strippers Hall of Fame, 8

Takeda, Isamu, 85
Texas Pharmacy Museum, 61
Thelen, David, 5, 31, 38, 49, 112–
    113
Tony Polito's Barber Shop and Military
    Museum, 6, 85
tourism and tourists, 57, 108–109;
    growth of, 30, 98; international,
    105–108; studies, 10
Travelers Club and International Tuba
    Museum, 82

The Unknown Museum, 50–51
Urry, John, 103

Valueland, 86, *88*
vernacular exhibition. *See* exhibits
Victoria Station, 78
visitor studies, 9
visitors, 4, 30, 37, 41–42, 52–57, 67, 77, 93–96, 102–110, 114

Washington County Farm Museum, 67
Wells Fargo History Museum, 21

West, Patricia, 37
Wetlians, Howard, 104
Windy Hollow Restaurant and Museum, 84
World of Coca-Cola, 21–22
Wright Museum of African American History, 20–21

Da Yoopers Tourist Trap and Museum, 1–4, 30, 67–70, 108

About the Author

Tammy S. Gordon is assistant professor of history at the University of North Carolina, Wilmington. She worked as an exhibits assistant and later was Assistant Curator of Exhibits at the Michigan State University Museum. She holds a Ph.D. in American Studies with an emphasis on social and cultural history and teaches graduate courses in public history, museum exhibition, and museum education.